MW01286763

The
COMPLETE
PARANORMAL
INVESTIGATION
HANDBOOK

The
COMPLETE
PARANORMAL
INVESTIGATION
HANDBOOK

A Comprehensive Guide for Ghost Hunters

RICHARD PALMISANO & PETER J. ROE

LLEWELLYN
WOODBURY, MINNESOTA

First Edition
First Printing, 2025

Book design by Christine Ha
Cover design by Kevin R. Brown

Llewellyn Publications is a registered trademark of Llewellyn Worldwide Ltd.

Library of Congress Cataloging-in-Publication Data
Names: Palmisano, Richard author | Roe, Peter J., 1969- author
Title: The complete paranormal investigation handbook : a comprehensive guide
  for ghost hunters / by Richard Palmisano and Peter J. Roe.
Description: First edition. | Woodbury, MN : Llewellyn Publications, [2025]
  | Includes bibliographical references. | Summary: "Whether you're a
  novice or part of an established team, this book will enhance your
  paranormal investigation skills. Featuring groundbreaking theory and
  strategies to look at old problems in new ways, this book is the key to
  conducting professional and science-based field studies"– Provided by
  publisher.
Identifiers: LCCN 2025007608 (print) | LCCN 2025007609 (ebook) | ISBN
  9780738777344 paperback | ISBN 9780738777412 ebook
Subjects: LCSH: Ghosts–Research–Methodology
Classification: LCC BF1461 .P35 2025 (print) | LCC BF1461 (ebook) | DDC
  133.1–dc23/eng/20250515
LC record available at https://lccn.loc.gov/2025007608
LC ebook record available at https://lccn.loc.gov/2025007609

Llewellyn Publications
A Division of Llewellyn Worldwide Ltd.
2143 Wooddale Drive
Woodbury, MN 55125-2989
www.llewellyn.com

Printed in the United States of America

GPSR Representation:
UPI-2M PLUS d.o.o., Medulićeva 20, 10000 Zagreb, Croatia,
matt.parsons@upi2mbooks.hr

Other Books by Richard Palmisano

Ghosts: An Investigation into a True Canadian Haunting

Ghosts of the Canadian National Exhibition

*Journeys into the Unknown: Mysterious
Canadian Encounters with the Paranormal*

Meeting Place of the Dead: A True Haunting

*Overshadows: An Investigation into a
Terrifying Modern Canadian Haunting*

Other Books by Peter J. Roe

Haunted Town Halls: From the Case Files of The Searcher Group

In memory of
Patricia Taylor Farley
1946–2020
Missed and never forgotten
—

CONTENTS

INTRODUCTION

*The boundaries which divide Life from
Death are at best shadowy and vague.
Who shall say where the one ends,
and where the other begins?*
—Edgar Allan Poe

This book is designed to be a comprehensive companion for those beginning their quest for answers into the human condition after death, as well as for the more seasoned researchers and investigators of paranormal phenomena seeking to expand their perspectives and improve upon the quality of their work. You are holding a compendium of a near half century of personal field experience and original theory designed to teach and (hopefully) inspire your own ideas and experimentation. The goal is not to prove ghosts exist but to advance humankind's knowledge of what to expect after we leave our physical bodies.

Before we get started, a couple of introductions are in order.

Richard Palmisano worked in law enforcement, security, and surveillance for thirty-seven years. During that time, he acquired and honed many of the skills necessary to aid in paranormal investigations, gaining invaluable experience conducting complex criminal investigations, collecting evidence, and using electronic surveillance techniques. Additionally, Richard has authored manuals for large corporations and government facilities. These include an operational security and procedural manual for Bell Canada Enterprise/Brookfield, Chief of Security, United Nations (NY), a security manual of emergency preparedness and emergency response for Ontario Lottery and Gaming, and a manual for Sun Life Canada, Security Operations.

Raised in a haunted house, Richard became fascinated with the paranormal at an early age. At eighteen years old, he launched The Searcher Group (TSG) in 1979, making it Canada's oldest paranormal investigation company. Its mission is to investigate paranormal activity, develop and conduct experiments for the advancement of parapsychology, and research and forge new technologies and theoretic models. Furthermore, The Searcher Group provides, free of charge, assistance to people having difficulty with paranormal activity either personally, in their home, or at their business. In 2011, Richard founded the Canadian Institute of Parapsychology, dedicated to education regarding life after death, ghosts, and hauntings.

Richard's published works include *Overshadows: An Investigation into a Terrifying Modern Canadian Haunting*; *Journeys into the Unknown: Mysterious Canadian Encounters with the Paranormal*; *Ghosts: An Investigation into a True Canadian Haunting*; *Ghosts of the Canadian National Exhibition*; *Meeting Place of the Dead: A True Haunting*; "Ghost of a Chance," an article for *The Skeptic – Quarterly Journal of Australian Skeptics* (March 2020); and "The Problem with the Paranormal" for the *Chicago Tribune*, April 2020. Several of Richard's works have been featured in internationally televised documentaries including the first season of *A Haunting* (*Overshadows*), *Northern Mysteries* (*Overshadows*), and *Portal into the Unknown* (*Ghosts* and *Ghosts of the Canadian National Exhibition*). The Searcher Group has also been featured in the *United Church Observer* (now *Broadview*) and *Reader's Digest*.

Though Peter J. Roe cannot claim to have had a direct paranormal experience as Richard did, the roots of his intrigue regarding ghost phenomena also began in childhood; reading of real-life haunted places around the world, followed by the exploits of Harry Price, Peter Underwood, and Hans Holzer, fueled his interest to someday join the quest. After participating in a ghost walk three decades later, Peter's appreciation for history and its overt connection to ghosts was cemented. On his mission to find a reputable team to work with, Peter discovered Richard's 2006 publication, *Journeys into the Unknown*. Impressed by original theory shared at the back of the book, Peter arranged to interview Richard—during which he felt *himself* being reviewed. After a series of months cutting his teeth investigating the grounds of the Canadian National Exhibition in 2010, Peter was formally invited to join The Searcher Group. He was appointed the role of assistant director soon afterward, contributing to the team website, promoting lectures, and arranging new field studies. Beginning in 2015, Peter spearheaded a thirty-month-long town hall tour, leading the team to conduct experimental, short-term field studies through southwestern Ontario. The exciting results of this experience became the basis of his debut publication, *Haunted Town Halls: From the Case Files of The Searcher Group*.

When the home office of The Searcher Group moved across Ontario in 2018, Peter was encouraged to undertake the role of director of TSG's inaugural subdivision. With a nod to *Hamlet*, Peter dubbed his team Mortal Coil Paranormal and continues to serve the greater Toronto area and southwestern Ontario, answering invitations to investigate and conducting public lectures year-round.

Peter has appeared on-screen in a testimonial capacity over two seasons of the Travel Channel's *Fear the Woods* and has been interviewed for CBC Radio, the Paranormal UK Radio Network, Night Fright Radio, two *Crash Course in Awesome* podcast episodes, two film documentaries, the *United Church Observer*, and *Reader's Digest*, among others.

* * *

An important question for everyone considering entering the world of paranormal investigation in a professional capacity is: How sure are you that this is something you want for yourself?

This field must be taken incredibly seriously and the work involved treated with the utmost respect. Some people interested in taking up this pursuit will argue all they need to get started are the gadgets they see on television, a video camera, and an atmospheric site to spend a few hours in. Screaming and running away in response to encountering paranormal phenomena is not acceptable, nor is trespassing or trashing a jobsite out of boredom or frustration when nothing spooky happens. That is the behavior of vandals and thrill- and fame-seekers, not true investigators.

As with exploring anything unknown, there are very real pitfalls and consequences a paranormal investigator may experience while conducting this line of work—even when off duty. You may receive a visit in your own home by someone—or something—you unwittingly encounter while scrutinizing a haunted location. This *could* happen even after your first attempt.

Take a moment to consider your friends, family, and, indeed, your pets. Even if you deem yourself strong and brave enough to handle unpredictable advances of an unseen force in your personal space, can you honestly say the same for your closest loved ones?

Ghosts have existed beyond time immemorial, and while some are not aware of their ethereal circumstance, many of them are aware they can expand their respective abilities. Don't for a moment think some won't resort to assailing a vulnerable family member or pet in order to weaken your resolve and force you to discontinue your investigative work. The attack may be physical or psychological in nature—in some cases, maybe both! Ask yourself if this is a repercussion you are willing to risk subjecting your loved ones to.

Apart from the very real dangers involved, this field of study also offers its own rewards. By this, we don't mean fame, adoration, and money, which are likely common endgames for the countless inspired by reality TV. Unless a professional investigation team is fortuitous enough to have its equipment and travel needs sponsored by a wealthy benefactor, there is no money to be made performing this line of work. (For the record, none of the royalties made back on any of the books we have labored to publish, nor honorariums gifted for guest testimonial appearances on TV shows, have even come close to compensating personal funds spent on gear, batteries, car fuel, insurance, and travel expenses.)

The rewards we reap conducting this work are far less material. Instead, they are feelings of wonderment when an unseen force activates a proximity meter or motion detector. They are the goose bumps that form when hearing disembodied footfalls, a voice addressing us in the moment, or an unmistakable electronic voice phenomenon (EVP) recording responding directly to an investigator's question. They are the chills of a discarnate touch or of witnessing an inanimate object move, seemingly under its own power. They are the satisfaction that your efforts have confirmed or even resolved a paranormal issue for your anxious clients. The *ultimate* reward is the feeling of an incredible sense of achievement when enough field data has accrued to posit a viable working theory toward explaining aspects of life-after-life phenomenon itself.

The search to discover answers to what lies beyond the end of physical life cannot possibly advance without ongoing discussion. The discussion itself must cease to rehash old, unproven theory, and its participants must be open to considering new ideas, experimentation, and cooperative peer review.

As you dedicate yourself to wading deeper into the intricacies of this line of research, we ask you to maintain a healthy skepticism, keep your mind open to many more possibilities beyond researching ghost phenomena, and exercise your patience as you explore the reams of information that await you. Maintaining a sense of humor will also keep the most serious researchers grounded.

Legitimate paranormal investigation and research involves a lot of work and knowledge going into it, so before you decide whether to read further, be certain that this journey is something you are truly prepared to embark on.

—Peter Roe, Assistant Director,
The Searcher Group (2011–present)

Why This Book Was Written

There are several reasons for this book. To start, it is to show the importance of history within paranormal research. This is a deep look into our past and the study of those who have lived and died. It's a study of the human condition, acknowledging the things they did, endured, and sometimes kept secret. The goal is to discover their stories through communication and research, examine that information, and apply it to our understanding of not only history but the afterlife.

Learn to question everything—even the old written-in-stone theories. Shake off all expectations and experience. Don't squeeze potential experiences into a ready-made mold, but build your own ideas and theories through deduction, reason, and logic.

We have great hope that this book will assist in the success of paranormal investigators and researchers everywhere. We are not talking about money or fame but truly finding and making progress in this field of study. Every advancement made is a step closer to solving this greatest of mysteries.

One of the major truths of paranormal phenomena is that it is tied to locations that were significantly important to the people of the past. Those ties were formed and bonded through emotion and familiarity. These locations can provide a researcher the best possible venues to study this phenomenon. Access to these significant properties, through the generosity of property managers and owners, provides the opportunity to make important discoveries in research, build theory, and bring us closer to solving this mystery.

It isn't just the investigators and researchers who become excited about new discoveries; it becomes a moment of excitement and pride for the property owners and managers, too. When something new is found on their properties, they know they had a part in bringing the information forward. These achievements could never happen without their help.

Born from over four decades of trial, error, and firsthand field experience, this book illustrates how you—as a professional investigator—can successfully (and respectfully) elicit those stories while contributing to meaningful advancements in this area of age-old wonder.

In short, we need to raise the bar of investigation standards if we are to have any hope of advancement. This book represents that bar.

History and ghosts go hand in hand; to speak of history is to examine and acknowledge those who once lived and built that history. Even in death they still have stories to share with us.

—Richard Palmisano,
Founder, Theorist, Director,
The Searcher Group (1979–present)

The Making of a Paranormal Investigator

The turn of the millennia introduced a fresh generation of ghost investigators influenced by TV paranormal shows such as *Most Haunted* with Yvette Fielding and *The Scariest Places on Earth* with Linda Blair. Then came *Ghost Hunters* with Jason Hawes and Grant Wilson of The Atlantic Paranormal Society (TAPS) in 2004 and *Ghost Adventures* in 2008 with Zak Bagans, Nick Groff, and Aaron Goodwin. A slew of similar television shows followed and continue to this day. Regarded as a new pastime, seeking spirits looked cool and scary and seemed easy: Simply buy some equipment from a ghost-hunting store (that suddenly appeared online), choose a spooky location (often privately owned), and go find a ghost.

We wish it were that simple; however, there is a great deal more to researching and investigating this type of phenomenon. Paranormal research and investigation is a discipline, involving years of study, learning, and conducting one's fieldwork properly.

Basic requirements that must be met to become a true paranormal investigator include an understanding of physiology, how human memory works, how the human eye operates and perceives things, how human hearing works, how sight and hearing work for domesticated animals, how the human body senses different environments, how the human mind works, how the mind perceives reality, and what brain patterns reveal to us, for starters.

Having a firm grasp on the fundamentals of parapsychology, spiritualism, and paranormal research is another must. All too often we encounter groups (and podcast hosts) whose education on the subject is based solely on what they've consumed through television. Mindfulness of the past, as well as keeping up to date on terminology in science and parapsychology, is incredibly important.

On the technical front, knowledge of each piece of your field equipment is also essential. How does it operate? What are the recommended uses, limitations, and operational parameters? What do the readings actually mean, and what might influence those readings? Are you able to distinguish a true reading or measurement from a false positive?

In terms of audio- and visual-capturing gear, are you familiar with photographic techniques? How about the uses, techniques, and limitations of surveillance systems? How about audio equipment? What about software systems that enhance photos, film, and sound? Are you proficient when analyzing audio and video recordings? Familiar with two-way radio systems?

What about investigation sites in terms of construction and building materials? Is someone on the team acquainted with knowledge of electricity? Air flow? HVAC systems? Thermal heating? Expansion and contraction phenomena? Fire safety and first aid? Common hazards and dangerous materials?

As for the investigation itself, are you and your team members well-versed in law-enforcement techniques such as investigation and interview methodology? How about the collection, handling, and preservation of evidence? Are there members of the team with a penchant for drawing floor plans of the study site? What about detail-heavy and timely report-writing? Does your team include a member or two who are aware of previous theories concerning paranormal phenomena, with an ability to conceptualize new theory based on data and field observations? Are they able to conceive and construct original experiments, test them in the field, and document the results?

Of course, we cannot possibly be taken seriously without human empathy and an understanding of logic, the grieving mind, and how emotions work, and also of more tangible elements such as temperature change, humidity, thermal climb, frequencies, acoustics, resonance, standing waves, mathematics, weights, measurements, electromagnetic fields, and the visual, ultraviolet (UV), and infrared (IR) spectra.

If you're still interested in seriously advancing this field, read on.

Principles That Are Extremely Useful to the Investigator

It is important for the investigator to enter an investigation with an open mind, to never jump to conclusions or build preconceived expectations. Look to the natural before contemplating the supernatural.

Occam's Razor

Scientific rule states that if you have two competing ideas to explain the same phenomenon, you should prefer the simpler one. A good investigator should employ this principle while starting an investigation, in the attempt to discover if what has occurred is of natural or paranormal origin.

Example: A client complains of hearing odd sounds in their attic and fears they have a ghost. Is it possible their attic is haunted, of course; however, the sounds are more likely to be caused by nesting birds, small animals or rodents, or even a damaged roof turbine vent. The point is: There are so many naturally occurring things that may be the cause for the sounds, and the investigator must eliminate all natural phenomena before looking for a paranormal explanation.

Critical Thinking

Critical thinking means making reasoned judgments that are logical and well thought-out. It is a way of thinking in which you don't simply accept all arguments and conclusions you are exposed to but rather have a mindset that will question such arguments and conclusions.

Identify what the problem or complaint is. Try to acquire specific information regarding the problem and move away from generalizations. Once the problem is clearly identified, only then can we start to discover why the problem exists and how it may be solved. Collect all available information on the issue through investigation and research. In many cases, we may have to engage several solutions in the attempt to resolve the problem. You may find there is more than one solution. Through analysis, however, you may find one is superior to the others.

Being objective is a fundamental part of critical thinking. That means analyzing the problem without allowing personal bias, emotions, or assumptions to influence how you think. A strong critical thinker will only analyze a problem based on the context and facts collected *after* conducting thorough and impartial research.

Collecting evidence is *the* primary goal of paranormal investigation.

When paranormal evidence is compared to evidence within the justice system, something amazing happens. Despite reams of credible, verifiable evidence collected over the last two centuries, the skeptic, the scientist, and sometimes even the parapsychologist will tell you there is no confirmation for life after death. Audio recordings can be subjective, photographic and video surveillance can be faked, and eyewitness accounts are worthless due to how we remember things and outside influences. In other words, if you were a criminal and they were the judge, you would never, ever do jail time.

We admit what they are saying can be true, and it all boils down to ethics and the sources from which the claims are coming from. Evidence of any kind must be handled and preserved properly. Evidence itself isn't just one thing; it is a collection of data points that support each other and tell a story. Be it a murder case, a fraud case, or a paranormal investigation, the collection of evidence is always the same.

Physical evidence involves any items that can assist in the uncovering of the story you are investigating. Every piece of evidence collected is considered circumstantial.

Footprints, scratch marks, the stacking of items, spontaneous fires, the manipulation of the physical environment, and other such things should all be documented. If photos of evidence are to be taken, then do so before anything is touched or moved. Pay special attention to anything that materialize out of thin air, which is known as an *apport*. This has been known to happen during hauntings and, in particular, poltergeist events. Examples include the sudden appearance of small pebbles, coins, keys, religious items, and even old medical bandages. These items should be photographed and secured inside a sealed envelope or container with all pertinent data recorded, including the time and date the object was found, specific location, type of object, marks, writing or dates on the object, their specific description and condition, and a summary that describes how the object came into the team's possession.

Example of Supported Evidence

An example from one of our investigations demonstrates how pieces of information collected and tied together form a basis of evidence. We had recorded a clear EVP of a male saying, "They are here, Miriam." Interesting. Weeks later, a visiting medium touring the property mentioned an older spirit of a woman named Miriam. Further into the investigation, the property owners showed us old newspapers and magazines—once used as insulation—found inside a wall of the investigation site during renovations. They ranged from 1905 to 1907, and on the mailing labels was the name Miriam. Not one of these things alone is evidence of anything; however, *together* they all reinforce each other as evidence.

Photography

Any type of camera can produce results—as long as you follow some rules. The camera must be in good working order, and you should be familiar with how everything works. Keep the camera clean and free from dust. When using the camera, watch for light sources; they may cause a lens flare and mislead you into thinking you've captured a true anomaly. Lamps, lights, sun, and flash bounce can all cause an image flare. Rain, snow, moisture, and dust particles can all reflect light, especially from a camera flash. Control your camera strap and lens cover; don't let them fall in front of the lens. If you have long hair, you may want to tie it back or wear a hat. Be aware that if you take photos toward shiny or reflective surfaces, they will produce a glare or reflection from your flash (or other light sources). When more than one investigator is photographing in an area, be sure to communicate with the others so you are not overlapping flashes into someone else's photos. If you are shooting photos outdoors, especially at night, try to include an object in the background to allow for a size and distance comparison. Without a sense of scale, an open-air photo at night is almost impossible to orient yourself to. If it is cold, be aware of the steam your breath will make, mist, or fog. Never smoke anywhere near where you are shooting photographs, and in the summer, watch for fireflies, which can give the illusion of slow-moving, flashing orbs.

Field Experiments

When delving into this complex field of research and discovery, we must question *everything* about the work that has been done and compiled over the last one hundred and fifty years—everything. It is up to each of us to examine that work and question old theories. It is the greatest pitfall to take these theories as gospel and try to fit your experiences and findings into them. Make these theories work for your trust. How do they apply to what you have found or discovered? Do they make sense? Do they work, knowing what we know today? We bring this up because even the best, most popular theories sometimes don't make sense or are not consistent.

Let's look at the Stone Tape theory, for example. The first person to suggest this idea was Thomas Charles Lethbridge (1901–1971) in the United Kingdom; he was an archaeologist, parapsychologist, and explorer in the 1900s. Lethbridge believed that residual hauntings may be recordings imprinted on the physical environment. His theory became popular due to a fictional TV film made by the BBC called *The Stone Tape* (1972).

It is a fairly simple theory. A highly emotional event is recorded by some unknown means and by some unknown medium and—when some activator is present—the event will replay like a visual memory projection or hologram. And yet we have seen absolutely zero advancements or discoveries on this theory over the last sixty years. Possibly, unlocking this mystery is like unlocking a combination lock; there are only so many variables to consider, such as the emotional state of the investigator or the use of a medium; possible solar flares, weather conditions, or geomagnetic storms; the specific frequency of a human voice, cell phone, or other piece of equipment; and maybe the relationship between the earth and moon. We have tried using a frequency generator and tuning forks, applied extreme pressure on some of the stone at this haunted location, and even sent electrical charges through the rock—and nothing. No manifestations. Nothing to indicate any type of haunting. So, perhaps we can't unlock this mystery because there is no such thing as the Stone Tape phenomenon!

It is important to remember to ask questions, even if you think you know the answer. Sometimes asking questions and receiving opinions and insights can lead the investigator to develop new ways of looking at a problem.

Chapter 1
INVESTIGATION BASICS

We cannot presume that most ghost enthusiasts reading this manual are arriving with extensive knowledge of ghost phenomena, types of hauntings, theories, or even why some people believe they have experienced an encounter with a ghost. With this in mind, we'll begin our deep dive into this fascinating world by discussing investigation basics—information that every professional investigator should know before undertaking an actual investigation.

Acknowledgment of the Term *Paranormal*

No discussion pertaining to studying and researching ghost phenomena is complete without reference to or direct involvement with some of the many topics that fall under the definitions of *unexplainable*, *supernatural*, or *paranormal*.

In the field of parapsychology alone, you'll find psi phenomenon, psychokinesis, extrasensory perception and mediumship, precognition, telepathy, out-of-body experiences, astral projection, psychometry, remote viewing, life after death, apparitions of the living and the dead, hauntings, spirit communications, electronic voice phenomena, dowsing, near-death experiences, reincarnation, spirit photography, spirit possession, and miracles.

We also wish to acknowledge additional paranormal topics, including ufology, cryptozoology, alternative human origins, magic, occultism, and anything outside the normal understanding of science. Though these additional subjects will not be discussed here, the protocols and disciplines outlined in this advanced manual can certainly be applied to investigators delving further into those areas of interest.

As long as we're being open-minded about the existence of ghosts, those of us researching ghost phenomena must also be prepared to continuously learn something of these other branches of the paranormal in connection. Find learning institutions with faculties that publish their ongoing parapsychology studies, and stay updated on the latest discoveries of quantum science.

We make many of these associations in the pages ahead. Perhaps you will discover more and write theory of your own. Perhaps you will have an opportunity to design and execute field tests. Perhaps you'll solve any number of conundrums that have eluded humankind, at once.

A Forewarning

When deciding to be an investigator, one must have some understanding of the type of problems that currently exist so as to avoid these pitfalls.

Finding a suitable location to conduct investigations and experiments is a difficult task. Gaining access is even harder. The site has to contain activity, be accessible, and provide an environment that can be, for the most part, controllable. These are all difficult criteria to meet. Finding the right place is even more difficult when you factor in thousands of paranormal groups clambering for access to every reputed haunted location on the planet; competition has become fierce, and we have discovered that many potential opportunities to attain data have been denied us by property owners who are unfamiliar with differences in professionalism.

The other major problem is finding people who are serious and devoted enough to such work to build a professional network. Collaboration is next to impossible. Our hope is that this manual will change that for the better.

Even the introduction of new theory, which is rare in itself, is not garnering any real attention from academics. Many teams are afraid to step away from the veteran path, and most are unsure of how to even test theory, opting instead to embrace a lot of the old theories despite many that have since been proven incorrect.

For a field of inquiry that demands open minds, sadly, many minds are shut tight.

What We Can Face as We Take This Journey

As investigators, we understand that "extraordinary claims require extraordinary evidence," as pointed out by Carl Sagan.[1] Neither the scientist nor the skeptic will settle for anything less, and neither should we. Before we look at all of this as a hopeless cause, we have to understand where skeptics and scientists are coming from. Most will create one-off explanations for the phenomena of ghostly activity, which by themselves could make some sense but automatically fail when scrutinized in field conditions. Examples of scientific explanations include:

Electromagnetic fields: According to Healthline.com, possible symptoms that people may experience when exposed

. . . .
1. Tressoldi, "Extraordinary Claims Require Extraordinary Evidence."

to electromagnetic energy fields (EMF) include loss of concentration, headaches, tremors, dizziness, memory loss, and sleep disturbance.[2] The presence of EMF has also been cited as an explanation for people's ghost experiences by American Canadian neuroscientist Michael Persinger (1945–2018), who studied the effects of electromagnetic fields, including the feeling of a presence in the lab with them.

With inventor Stanley Koren, Dr. Persinger created a device called the God Helmet, a weak EMF-emitting device that, when worn by subjects over a period of fifteen to thirty minutes under laboratory conditions, caused these perceptions.

As modern civilization finds itself completely surrounded by EMF emitted by cell towers, radio, power lines, Wi-Fi, and household appliances, Dr. Persinger's conclusion seemed reasonable. That was, until Richard personally asked him how this theory applied to people seeing ghosts a hundred years ago or even a thousand years ago. He didn't have an answer. So much for extraordinary claims requiring extraordinary evidence.

Infrasound: Infrasound consists of low frequency vibrations generated by off-balanced fans, wind, thunder, and even atmospheric pressure, for example. These vibrations are known to cause physiological discomfort and can also cause disorientation, feelings of uneasiness or panic, chills down the spine, changes in heart rate and blood pressure, nausea, vomiting, and bowel spasms.

. . . .

2. Cirino and Lamoreux, "Should You Be Worried About EMF Exposure?"

Mold: If you enter a location with mold present (including someone's home, a publicly accessible building, or abandoned structure), then there is a chance you and your team may be exposed to it. Obvious cautions aside, while mold is often blamed for people seeing and hearing ghosts, feeling irrational fear, and even experiencing dementia, there has been no link established to say this is a cause for experiencing ghostly phenomena.

Carbon monoxide: Carbon monoxide poisoning may occur anywhere an indoor investigation takes place. Carbon monoxide can cause agitation, confusion, depression, lethargy, impulsiveness, distractibility, memory problems, and aural and visual hallucinations. As investigators, we cannot definitively point to a paranormal explanation until all naturally occurring phenomena has been ruled out first.

Alleged shared experience: If someone can be so convincing that they saw a ghost, they could potentially make other people present in the moment believe they saw one, too.

Confirmation bias: When someone so powerfully wants to believe that they will see a ghost, there is a possibility that they will convince their brain that they have indeed had that experience.

Grief: Similar to confirmation bias, people experiencing extreme anguish and mental suffering are also likely to convince themselves they see the deceased person (or people). Science believes this is a brain function that assists us in dealing with painful and traumatic events.

Fear: Some people can place themselves in such an extreme state of fear that their mind plays tricks on them, where every sound no longer has a natural explanation, to the extent they take a posture of fight or flight. At that point, they will genuinely believe they have had a paranormal encounter.

Illness or drugs: Schizophrenia and dementia can lead to people hearing voices and seeing apparitions. Similarly, the use of heavy drugs may also cause hallucinations.

Geomagnetic phenomena: Science has suggested that geological phenomena may cause the illusion of ghostly activity. Alterations in geomagnetic activity or disturbances of the planet's magnetosphere could cause temporary changes within our brains. There is very little evidence to support this hypothesis.[3]

Seizures: Research conducted by Dr. Persinger also suggests that seizures occurring in the temporal lobes may induce perceptions of ghostly encounters.[4]

Sleep paralysis: This condition, in which the mind has woken and the body has not, makes it so that the body cannot move. Known as atonia, it may cause hallucinations, though science hasn't clearly explained why the brain might hallucinate at this time.

Pareidolia (a.k.a. matrixing): Pareidolia is a brain phenomenon where we try to create meaningful explanations out of random or ambiguous images or sounds. Examples include seeing faces or familiar shapes in cloud formations, an image of the Virgin Mary on a piece of toast, or a smiling face on the surface of Mars.

Hallucinations: While carbon monoxide, drugs, and sleep paralysis may be behind people experiencing vivid

....

3. Persinger, "My Tectonic Strain Theory Is Alive and Well."
4. Persinger, "The Neuropsychiatry of Paranormal Experiences."

hallucinations, medical/psychological issues such as high anxiety, depression, and stress are other factors to consider as well.

Most of the items on this list can very easily be resolved by examination using specific equipment and meters and a thorough inspection of the area. What science-based, one-off explanations *don't* account for are eyewitness and mechanical corroboration, such as people seeing an apparition that is simultaneously being recorded on camera. The reason this information is important to consider is that beyond those who have a deep interest in the paranormal who may wish to see your work, there are also those who wish to see your work debunked and fail. As professionals, we need to include all groups in our work and show everyone why what we bring forward has merit.

Dynamics of a Haunting

When investigating a location, you should consider that people who live there currently and people who have lived there in the past all have the potential to return to that location after death. For each person who dies and has a deep-seated connection to the location, the potential for them to return and influence the activity that is reported warrants consideration. Any time a new spirit is added to a location, the noted activity can change. The addition of a new spirit may form a type of balance, reducing the phenomenon, or incite a conflict, creating greater activity. In some situations, it will end the activity all together. In many cases, we hear from clients that the haunting has changed (more aggressive, higher activity, etc.), and thus discovering the recent death of a previous inhabitant is all the more important.

The amount of research required can be staggering, and the success for an undertaking of this magnitude is only measured by the commitment of the investigator. The older the location is and the more it has changed ownership will increase the amount of research work required.

Things to consider include researching anyone who previously lived at the location and is deceased, including previous owners and their children, extended family members, staff and servants, and renters and tenants. Some of the unknowns include any attachments to the land previous to the structure being built, any attachments to persons or items brought into the location, any rituals or spirit board sessions that may have occurred there, and any transient spirits attracted to the location.

Some problems may occur when researching women in history prior to the 1970s, as you may encounter difficulty discovering their birth names. Married women often took on their husband's name and lost their identity, such as Mrs. John Smith. This becomes a bit of a nightmare when the man was married more than once. You may have several Mrs. John Smiths connected to the same person, and it can be difficult to determine which woman was the first wife and so on.

Cross-examining birth, death, and census records is the ideal way to begin to fill in the big picture.

Thoughts on What Ghosts Could Be

Ghosts are known by many names worldwide, and there are just as many theoretical explanations posited by physical people regarding what they are exactly. Here are six ideas that most students of ghost study are likely already familiar with:

Spirits of dead people: Ghosts could be the soul or "essence" of the deceased that remain on the physical plane of reality and are attached to a specific place. Some believe in the existence of transient spirits, which are not attached to any specific location and have the ability to travel. Others postulate the ability of a spirit to connect to a specific object. (See the section "Haunted Objects and How to Utilize Them" in chapter 5.)

Interdimensional beings: Ghosts could possibly be interdimensional visitors, some being benevolent and others malevolent.

Recordings of the past: As proposed in the Stone Tape theory, ghosts could be nothing more than events recorded within an environment and played back by unwitting perceivers with mediumistic abilities. (See "The Stone Tape Theory Debunked: Synchronicity Within a Haunting" in chapter 8.)

Angels and demons: Ghosts may be perceivable manifestations of angels and demons interacting with and influencing the living.

Manifestations of the subconscious mind: Simply put, our subconscious mind may create phenomena (thought forms or tulpas) perceived either within our own imagination or possibly within a collective unconsciousness.

Hallucinations: Despite historical evidence to the contrary, there are a great number of scientists who believe ghostly phenomena is nothing more than hallucination brought on by any number of causes, including drugs, mold, high electromagnetic frequencies, and so on.

Standing Theories on Types of Spirits and Hauntings

The Searcher Group tends to balk at the classification of ghosts based on their respective abilities to manifest. We understand that humankind is quick to sort our outer world into neat, accessible patterns and categories. To us, however, a ghost-is-a-ghost-is-a-ghost. Why is a ghost that expresses itself angrily by making noise and moving physical objects labeled a "poltergeist" in one instance, when the week before the same spirit was called an "orb" when it was spotted briefly, emitting its own light? Or, when a spirit runs up and down the hall every day at noon, it's termed "residual energy," but when it slams a door in your face in response to an insult, it's considered "intelligent"?

Despite our objections to these characterizations, the world at large continues to utilize them. If we're going to speak the same language in this field, it's ideal if we are mindful of their definitions:

> *Residual haunting:* These hauntings are imprinted events that are attached to a specific place. The activity taking place cannot communicate or interact with the living and the observed activity cannot be changed. "Residual" hauntings are popularly considered to be the opposite of "intelligent" hauntings.

> *Anniversary haunting:* The activity that presents itself only occurs on a specific date and time of day and is believed to hold a very significant event or memory for the spirit, compelling it to "relive" that event.

> *Intelligent haunting:* These hauntings are caused by spirits that manipulate their surroundings, interact with the living, and communicate. Depending on their intent, they may behave in benevolent, malevolent, or simply mischievous manners.

Crisis apparition: This is the appearance of a person's spirit to friends or loved ones at or very near the time of that person's sudden or traumatic death. Crisis apparitions can also include thought forms that *appear* as ghosts to the perceiver but are actually projected by a living person undergoing some sort of trauma far from the manifested image event. (This second instance is not to be confused with the biologic-based doppelgänger phenomenon.)

Benevolent haunting: A benevolent haunting is caused by a spirit that is content to exist in simpatico with the living. These spirits may even come to the aid of their corporeal roommates if need be.

Malevolent haunting: These are caused by spirits that may cause harm to the living or, at the very least, resort to aggressive tactics in order to achieve their goals—usually to rid their space of the flesh-and-blood occupants. Other forms of malevolent hauntings include:

Poltergeists: Poltergeists are energetic forces that tend to manifest unexpectedly and disappear just as quickly, without logical rhyme or reason. A poltergeist infestation typically includes disembodied sounds, physical interactions (e.g., property damage, pinching/slapping/pushing), apport phenomena, psychological abuse, and—in rare cases—disembodied human voices. Compared to a standard, long-term haunting, poltergeist phenomena is limited to days, weeks, months, or a couple of years before ceasing.

Demonic/evil entities: Demonic or evil entities are dark forces that may or may not be of human origin that have the intention to cause great harm to the living.

Why Are They Here?

We must discover why ghosts are here, all around us. It seems that there isn't anywhere for them to go, as they exist in their own reality, which overshadows ours. Heaven and hell are not specific places but rather a frame of mind. Those places are what we create for ourselves for the time being. For those of us who pass over in peace, we move on to join dearly departed relatives that have gone on before us. For those not at peace, they create their own hell, fueled by fear, guilt, greed, and evil deeds committed in life. They become their own tormentors, clinging to the edges of reality in present time, dwelling and hiding, hoping they will not be seen for what they are. Several popular religions have painted horrible pictures of hell, and as a result, some spirit people truly believe that if they progress, a far worse fate awaits them.

As they exist in extremely close proximity to our own reality, they can pass through time and space into our reality. Their realties are based on frequencies different from our own. Science has shown us that everything has a specific frequency. Human life operates on several frequencies. In death, these frequencies are changed slightly, vibrating at a level that we cannot see or hear. When the spirit is laden with strong emotion—fear, guilt, helplessness, or wanting—these negative feelings send them into a depression, lowering these frequencies, and thus their actions start to manifest into our reality with sights, sounds, and odd smells. In life, it seems that our bodies act as insulators, like the rubber around an electrical wire. As we die and the body is shed, the spirit energy released is elevated in frequency.

Time Slips

There are some fascinating reports, from around the world, linking time slip phenomena with the presence of ghosts. A time slip is an alleged event by witnesses who feel they have been transferred to another time and have become embedded with an event in history. An earlier term for this is *retrocognition*.

Albert Einstein once wrote in 1955, at the loss of his friend Michele Besso, in a letter of condolence, "People like us who believe in physics know that the distinction between past, present and future is only a stubbornly persistent illusion."[5] The concept of time, in other words, is an illusion.

For example, Einstein's theory of special relativity proposes that time is an illusion that moves relative to an observer. This is fascinating. However, in the course of a perceived time slip event, what if the dominant observer is the *spirit* and not the living percipient?

When several spirits are all connected to a specific event, all remembering that event from different points of views (which seems to give the phenomena life and dimension), the spiritual consensus seems to support the time slip into our perceived reality, however briefly.

Time Slips and Battery Drainage

In instances where time slip phenomena is perceived to occur, many field investigators report significant energy drainage (or outright loss) from their electronic and electric-based equipment on a consistent basis. Naturally, the blame for this inexplicable circumstance has fallen on the presence of an entity (or group of entities) in the immediate vicinity. In this instance, a prevailing theory posits that an unseen ghost is purposely collecting this energy as a means to assist with manifesting themselves in order to be perceived by the living witness(es).

Looking at cases where this has happened, there is no evidence that the use of this energy ever assisted in a manifestation.

....

5. Mainwood, "Einstein Believed in a Theory of Spacetime That Can Help People Cope with Loss."

When a spirit and the living come together, it is possible that a time shift is occurring—more specifically, an overlap of the living's time in the present and that of the bygone era perceived by the spirit. The energy drain experienced by the living occurs because the ghost's time era dominates the moment and effectively supersedes the very *existence* of modern-day equipment, rendering it powerless. We base this theory on many field observations where batteries that appear to be completely depleted in the course of a paranormal encounter are miraculously restored once removed from the study area.

Social Spirits

Investigating ghosts for most of his life, Richard has always been fascinated with the social characteristics of spirits, how they act and interact with one another.

Richard first became aware of this interaction in 1996 when he investigated a home that entailed a multiple haunting. In this case, a teenage girl died by suicide and then returned home to discover her family had left and a new family had moved in. What she also found was that there were other spirits there. A conflict arose between the newly arrived teen spirit and a malevolent, dominating spirit named Edward, who had control over the home and other spirits. The young girl seemed to want none of this and a battle ensued, leaving the living family trapped between the spirits in a nightmare situation.

The action that took place between these two entities demonstrated to Richard that there was little difference in people's treatment of one another, no matter which side of existence they stood on. The activity was extremely negative, as Edward constantly pursued the girl throughout the house and property.

At first, Richard was led to believe it was purely a control issue, but as the investigation proceeded, he discovered it was much more than that. Control, yes, but also a quest for knowledge on Edward's part. Knowledge is power, after all. Edward, having died in the 1940s, demonstrated difficulty understanding our technology, and in the beginning, he gave us extraordinary evidence of his existence between video and audio surveillance. This all changed once Edward caught the girl and coerced her into teaching him how our modern-day cameras and cassette tape recorders worked. Once armed with this newfound knowledge, Edward tampered with our surveillance equipment.

Richard had to wonder if this social situation was unique. He had investigated many haunted locations, and not until 2003 did he get a second astonishing look at this kind of interaction. Richard was working a job in Mississauga, Ontario, involving two haunted houses sharing the same property.

Lewis and Elizabeth Bradley built their farmhouse in 1830; the home today is a museum operated by the city of Mississauga. The spirits there are friendly and welcoming. Also resting on the Bradley property is a relocated house known as the Anchorage—a fine example of Regency-style construction. It was owned by Commander John Skynner, who served under Admiral Horatio Nelson aboard his ship *Hirondelle* and battled against France and its emperor, Napoleon. Skynner settled into his home in its original location in 1839. Although Commander Skynner and the Bradleys were separated by class distinction, they all were part of the same small community known as Merigold's Point.

The reports at the Anchorage were of strange noises, lights that turned on and off without reason, doors that would close on their own, and staff who reported dizziness and nausea.

We had just finished shooting interviews for the Discovery Channel documentary series *A Haunting* (an episode entitled "Darkness Follows," loosely based on Richard's first book, *Overshadows*) at the

Bradley Museum, and Richard and his brother Paul were taking a break outside. Paul shared that he had seen two spirits near the rear of the old homestead. He described a man and a woman and the period clothing they were wearing. They mentioned this to the curator, who said Paul's description matched that of the Bradleys.

Our first investigation in the Skynner house was short; however, it showed us that the reports from staff were valid. We were all sitting in the meeting room on the main floor when Paul and Richard kept hearing creaking noises from the floor near the back door. Richard decided to respond by jumping out into the hall and firing his camera toward the back door. Framed in the windows of the door to the foyer were two ghostly images—a man looking through the left glass panel and a woman looking through the right panel, both wearing period clothing. Paul recognized the couple as the two spirits he had seen behind the Bradley house. When we showed the image to the curator, she came back with photos of the Bradley portraits; the similarities were startling.

We mused philosophically on what this photo meant. Could there be a social interaction between spirits? Had the Bradleys come over to see Skynner, or had they come over to investigate what we were doing here? Regardless, they were now visiting a house that did not sit on this patch of land until the 1970s. This meant that they were aware of its existence even though they were both dead long before it had been moved here. Could that mean they knew of and visited the commander as well? We believed so.

In Richard's third book, *Ghosts*, he explored the social interactions between the spirits that dwelt on this remarkable estate located in Mississauga. There we had the opportunity to pull back the proverbial veil and have a glimpse at these incredible afterlife relationships. Richard personally felt we'd made very profound discoveries:

For one, the lady of the house ordered a spirit butler named Henry to watch over and keep a male child named Danny under control and away from harm. For his part, Henry seemed to be run ragged chasing after Danny, barking out warnings and instructions. A servant spirit named Anna Rita continues her duties to this day, maintaining a stairwell, keeping it clean and polished. Additionally, the spirit of a young girl named Tonya would visit from a farmhouse on an adjacent property and play with Danny.

The spirits of children and servants between the farm and the mansion maintained a meaningful coexistence. I found it interesting that in all of these cases there exists a social interaction between spirits. To me it would seem that even in death, life goes on as if it was—or is—never truly interrupted.

Shadow People

As the focus on ghosts intensified throughout popular culture from the early 2000s on, one term was coined to describe another, albeit particularly chilling, kind of ghost manifestation: *shadow people*. These jet-black, featureless figures seem to fall between the "traditional" transparent shape and the solid, flesh-and-blood expressions ghosts can demonstrate at will or by skill.

Commonly sighted via one's peripheral vision (a.k.a. the corner of your eye) before fleeing, figures of shadow are rarely observed for very long by looking at them directly. However, several notable exceptions occurred while The Searcher Group undertook the Fusion Mansion case in Mississauga, Ontario (2005–08).

The very night the team was introduced to the property by a city employee, a solid black humanoid figure placed itself between Richard and Paul (who were standing several yards apart from each other) on a pathway just outside the mansion. At first confusing the figure for Paul (also clad in black), Richard had no time to gather his wits and point his camera toward the entity before it turned on its heel and disappeared behind a twenty-inch-wide tree trunk at incredible speed. Rattled both by the figure's stealth and cartoonlike departure, Paul and Richard soon compared their individual experiences—from Paul's angle, the figure was a luminescent white!

Over the three-year investigation period, several encounters with "shadow people" by multiple witnesses took place on the grounds of the property—all of them outside the mansion and nearby coach house, but the photo negative phenomenon that Richard and Paul experienced was not repeated. Just as fascinating, the dark entities darting about the trees and foliage were not only feared by the ghosts inside the mansion but could not be easily read by visiting mediums. Each psychic independently reported sensing a consciousness to these figures, but where thoughts, memories, and emotions would normally be conveyed by a human ghost, there was only a static-like void coming from these particular creatures of shadow.

The prevailing theory in this instance is that because cold fusion experiments were conducted on this particular property by provincial utilities supplier Ontario Hydro (now Hydro One) many years previously, the "shadow people" now inhabiting the grounds may be beings that entered our realm through a portal that was unwittingly opened in the process. (Going a step further, perhaps these creatures have adopted humanoid forms in an attempt to acclimate themselves among people as best they can?)

It is highly unlikely your team will encounter these same kinds of entities appearing as figures of shadow; however, this real-life experience is included here to illustrate (and remind us) that anything is possible.

The more commonly encountered "shadow person" that people are likely to witness is but a ghost who is demonstrating a specific stage in their manifestation abilities. Whether the ghost appears in shadow form because they are on their way to achieving the ability to form into a solid, full-color state or because they're actually becoming weaker from once having had the ability to appear as a normal flesh-and-blood person, we'll probably never discover.

An internet search for "shadow people" dredges up many sites that claim this form of ghost is a particularly malicious and evil entity. We suspect this assumption is based on two things: First, the inability to read a figure's facial expression if there are no discernible features visible is certainly disconcerting and would naturally trigger a flight response. Second, numerous television and feature film productions worldwide have incorporated shadowy appendages and figures as antagonistic and symbols of danger for years! How could one *not* feel threatened if suddenly in their presence?

Figures of shadow are also not limited to humans, as illustrated in CCTV surveillance footage Richard owns of a pair of running hounds (see "Determining Whether to Share" in chapter 7). People have reported seeing shadowy forms of cats, dogs, horses, bears, and birds as well.

Demons and Other Nonhuman Entities

Whatever you call them, the bad news is malevolent entities exist; the good news is that they are extremely rare. Even if encountered on an investigation, most of these entities want nothing to do with you unless your actions directly interfere with or interrupt their agendas.

Why do so many people believe that ghostly phenomena must be demonic?

The ideology comes from religious teachings out of Judaism, Christianity, and Islam that there are no ghosts, only demonic entities. Therefore, anything otherworldly that one comes into contact or communicates with is a demon by proxy. This attitude naturally accounts for many paranormal encounters that automatically fall into the realm of "demonic" activity.

To solidify this idea into the minds of the faithful, the Vatican says it has vigorously started hiring and training exorcists by the hundreds, insisting there is a need.[6] And yes, we understand the old argument—that demons are the construct of the church, created as a control—however, as investigators, we again cannot stress the importance of learning things such as history, where one can discover demons have been documented well before the church (or even Catholicism) ever existed, going back to ancient Sumeria and Egypt.[7]

Whether or not demons exist is to be determined. What we do know according to recorded data is that the majority of hauntings, including poltergeist events, rarely cause physical harm. They can be destructive to property and very frightening, but they stop short of causing critical injuries to the living. This is not to say ghosts cannot cause some harm, but typically it is minor.

On the spectrum of ghosts resides the spectrum of personalities of those once living, from the nicest and most kindhearted to the foulest psychopath. The consensus is: You are what you are personality-wise and death rarely changes that.

If any of these dark, diabolical entities are encountered, the investigation should cease immediately. Step back and monitor everyone involved for continued activity for three to four days after exiting the investigation site. If the activity does continue, consult with your specific religious group. If you are dealing with a nonhuman entity, now is not the time to play games by bringing in self-proclaimed demonologists, as things can go from bad to worse very quickly.

....

6. Sinneberg, "As Exorcism Demand Continues to Rise, Vatican to Hold Training."
7. Guiley, *The Encyclopedia of Demons and Demonology*.

Dynamics of a Diabolical Haunting

When a family unit begins to experience strange occurrences in their residence, various family members may at the onset keep those occurrences quiet for fear of sounding crazy. Several members may be experiencing happenings, yet there may be no communications until it becomes out of control and extremely frightening or two members experience something together, opening a dialogue.

In about 85 percent of hauntings in a residence, the female is first to notice these strange events; this can cause stress and extreme frustration within the family unit, as the male may not completely believe what the female is saying, having not had an experience himself. In some cases, this may be the ploy on the part of the haunter to divide and conquer.

In our group's experience, in 100 percent of all cases where pets are involved in the home, the pet will be fully aware of the presence within the residence and may display behavioral changes, such as looking at seemingly empty spaces, watching something humans can't see, growling, barking for no apparent reason, acting nervous or agitated, and exhibiting changes in eating habits.

Where a presence may be malevolent, the pet will likely become the first target, followed by the women in most cases.

Children can also be a target. However, the dynamics can be diabolical, as they may be befriended and appear to have an imaginary friend.

In the majority of hauntings, there is very little fear of injury. Rather, the haunters will normally have some sort of message or story to communicate. Most of these situations can be resolved.

However, in diabolical hauntings, nothing will be as it may appear. For example, a child apparition may not be a child at all, but something darker. Seeing things appearing exactly as someone you know or sounding like another family member indicates a more sinister situation. We've noted that in situations where pets are in the residence, there is a 75 percent chance that the pet will not survive the first six months of this type of haunting.

The investigator must try to distinguish the difference between a haunting where, for example, a spirit feels, "Hey, this is my house; I have the ability to scare you away!" and one where the entity's goal is destruction of the family unit.

Some of the weapons used by an entity in a diabolical haunting include quietly observing and gaining intelligence for a period of time or terrorizing your pets.

A diabolical entity may drive a psychological wedge between the primary couple by terrorizing one person and ensuring the other never has an experience. This will result in heightened fear as the target person starts to feel singled out and alone and may even question their very sanity. The unaffected person will start to experience poor sleep patterns and possible health issues and may question their partner's sanity, too. Arguments inevitably ensue due to the combined stresses, demonstrating that the entity can manipulate your child and pull them in specific directions or have them do things that make the other inhabitants feel they are in jeopardy.

If you love your house, a diabolical entity will turn it into a nightmare for you. The investigator must unify the family unit and show them that they must stand together and support one another.

Depending on the resources of the investigative team to attempt to resolve these hauntings, there will always remain the possibility that the only option for the family is to leave the house. Every possible option must be tried prior to making the decision to leave. This option cannot be taken lightly, as in most cases financial ruin of the family unit will likely result.

Is Human Memory Trustworthy?

As paranormal investigators and researchers, we do our due diligence and try to apply science and scientific methods to everything we do. Science does very well when dealing with the physical world but not so well when the field of study falls into the realm of the nonphysical. Science cannot explain the mind, consciousness, feelings, intuition, dreaming, or even why we sleep. It would seem mainstream science experiences a difficult time with memory as well.

When it comes to memory and recounting something we have seen or experienced, the proverbial court is undecided. After reviewing mountains of research papers published by specialists such as psychologists, neuroscientists, and biologists, we have found no definitive consensus.

A great deal of research shows that eyewitness testimony—when it comes to identifying a person or thing, regardless of how confident the eyewitness is—can be extremely unreliable. Studies show that when pressed for more information, an eyewitness will generate false details while truly believing their recollection is correct. Memory can be changed based on unconscious memory distortions and personal biases.

We recall a study (but sadly are unable to relocate its source) involving sixty-eight psychologists who all believed there would be a poor score within memory rates after a long delay. After their subjects were tested, they found the longer the delay, the fewer details witnesses recalled, but the details they did report were very accurate. Within the study, it was shown that there was a 93 percent accuracy rate, which was well above their estimates.

There are just as many papers that suggest our memories are extremely accurate. The one thing everyone does seem to agree upon is that memory is limited to a recall of about 22 percent of events, but of those events, the accuracy is about 94 percent.[8]

As a paranormal investigator, it is important to record information and experiences in a professional manner. Because memories can be brought into question, techniques used by police and security personnel should be used. As soon as you find a moment to document the information after an event, a highly detailed record should be made of what happened, including the exact location, who was involved, the time it occurred, and every detail connected to the event that you can recall. If this is a written report, draw a line at the conclusion and sign your name. This will signify the report is exactly as you wrote it and will indicate nothing can be added afterward. If the event is logged digitally, simply state your name at the end of the recording. This report will capture a moment in time when the details of an event are fresh in your mind.

Should you recall other details at another time or date, add this information to your report stating the new time and date of the entry, specifically noting that it is a "supplemental report."

Communicating with Spirits

The largest nonscientific setback to studying ghost phenomena is that the majority of our data is anecdotal in origin. As investigators, we deliberately place ourselves and our experiments on location in the hope that doing so will result in practical data provided to us by intelligent sources operating outside our perception. To the best of our current knowledge, here are the generally experienced clues that seen and unseen energies utilize, indicating they are very mindful and aware of their actions among us:

....

8. Diamond et al., "The Truth Is Out There."

Sensorial stimulation: Reports of a "heavy" sensation or an unexpected shift in emotion indicate the possible manifestation of a ghost's presence nearby. In addition to alerting one's intuitive feelings, unexplained olfactory phenomena is another common characteristic of an unseen energy. The sudden occurrence of smells ranging from pleasant (perfume, burning tobacco, flowers) to putrid (decay, urine, vomit) has also been described relating to spirit manifestations.

Raps and knocks: Impact sounds, such as knocking, raps, or scratching noises, with no obvious source of physical surfaces colliding with one another, are common.

Movement of items: People notice the deliberate physical movement of items, such as furniture, books, or anything else, by unknown forces without explanation.

Temperature: A rapid climb or drop in room temperature is believed to indicate that a spirit is attempting to manifest itself in some way.

Disembodied voices: Human utterances or sounds that are heard directly by the ear in real time and without a visible source have been documented. (This is not to be confused with electronic voice phenomena, which are primarily the *recordings* of *unheard* voices or sounds.)

Orbs: Eyewitnesses and investigators suggest spirits may appear as luminous, flying spheres of energy, while video and photograph analysts air strongly on the side of caution, citing dust particles, insects, and moisture droplets captured by cameras as the cause.

Partial manifestation: This is the observance of misty or smoky, translucent or shadowy figures that contain very few identifying details. The observer sometimes senses or feels it may be male or female.

Full-body or complete manifestation: This is a full-bodied apparition with great detail and the illusion of solidity that also displays a color such as black, gray, green, blue, and so on. An example is the Brown Lady of Raynham Hall. Still, while many report seeing a fully bodied figure, some ghosts will also manifest without a discernible face, head, or other appendages.

Ghosts and Physical Contact

You settle in for a long night of investigation at a historic property, which has a reputation of being haunted, when suddenly you feel a touch by something unseen.

The sensation sends information to your brain for an almost instant analysis and interpretation of what just happened. Something touched your arm, and yet there is nothing there that could have done this. How could this be?

So, is it possible that an unseen force may have touched you? We believe so.

Current physics experiments are showing that electromagnetic energy can move objects. The force they are experimenting with and observing is extremely weak. However, although they had believed this energy could push on an object, they have also found it can even pull on an object.[9]

These findings show that if spirits have anything to do with electromagnetic energy, well, the sky is the limit as far as manipulating their environment and ours.

. . . .
9. Muro, "Explainer."

Experimenting with Music

Music is a universal language that can trigger happy or sad feelings. It can elicit an increase in memory and emotion, which in turn can cause involuntary actions such as temperature changes, sounds, and voices and even allow various physical manifestations with regard to ghosts.

Scientific studies have demonstrated that music can evoke involuntary memories and cause an emotional response.[10] As investigators, we have observed that incorporating music during investigations can and will result in emotional responses from the dead. (See "The Trigger Effect" in chapter 7.)

Building experiments is one of the greatest projects an investigator can do, and it can involve eliciting an emotional response using music. However, to build such an experiment, the investigator must have some idea of who the haunter might be and the era during which they lived. This information will key the investigator into what meaningful piece of music to choose. After all, if the music choice isn't meaningful to the haunter, then chances are the investigator will receive no reaction.

Example: Richard used this method in a haunted location with great success. However, it took him more than a year to choose that right piece of music. After historical research and careful analysis of collected EVPs, Richard discovered a spirit child named Danny. The boy was safeguarded by a spirit caregiver who seemed to be overworked keeping watch over him. This caregiver spoke with a Scottish accent and quite often referred to the lad as "Danny Boy." It was at this time that Richard decided to play a recorded rendition of Frederic Edward Weatherly's "Danny Boy" (1913).

....
10. Hans-Eckhardt. "Music-Evoked Emotions—Current Studies."

In another instance, while performing archival research on a different location, Peter noted that one of the deceased residents was quite socially active within the community and had attended several parties and gatherings. A newspaper article even recounted that "Anna" (as the team had come to learn was the spirit's alleged name at the time) had performed a particular tune at one such gathering titled "Silver Threads Among the Gold" (1873). When a recorded version of this tune was played back during a follow-up investigation, Paul was heartbroken to discover an EVP had been captured by a nearby video camera of a woman sobbing pitifully at the song's conclusion. Whether they were tears of joy, gratitude, or sadness, we do not know, but music certainly provoked an audible manifestation, and "Anna" became a friend of the team in subsequent visits.

Mirrors

What is it about mirrors that can fascinate and frighten us?

They have been around for thousands of years in one form or another, and over time so many folktales and superstitions have developed around them. Going back to ancient times, mirrors were used to scry—a mystic's way of seeing distant places, people, and the future. A well-known alchemist, John Dee (1527–1608), used a mirror for scrying and advised Queen Elizabeth I of a plot to kill King James in 1605. The Romans believed that to break a mirror would bring bad luck for seven years.

After a death, some religious beliefs would command that the covering of mirrors be done to ensure the spirit of the deceased did not enter a mirror and become lost or trapped. In the Victorian era, mirrors had to be covered, clocks would be stopped at the moment of death, and the family would watch over the body without rest until the burial. This is where the term *wake* comes from. Medieval monks would place tiny mirrors on a small slender stick beside their noses so they could see spirits using their peripheral vision.

Staring into a mirror inside a room with very limited illumination can cause a person to see strange faces, animals, monsters, and deceased relatives. It may even expose their own soul. It is possible that this belief gave rise to vampires not having a reflection, as they would have no soul. Some legends claim that the act of *scrying*—gazing into a mirror in a darkened room with nothing more than a lit candle—will allow you to see spirits if they are present in your home.

A more elaborate version of scrying is called a psychomanteum, or apparition booth. This is a darkened room with a series of mirrors set up in a specific way to allow the viewer to see and even communicate with spirits. Raymond A. Moody Jr., PhD, MD, who termed the phrase *near-death experience*, discusses this at length in his 1993 book *Reunions: Visionary Encounters with Departed Loved Ones*.

Mirrors are also a large component in some contemporary urban legends, such as peering into a mirror and calling for Bloody Mary or Candyman several times.

Are Mirrors Portals for Ghosts?

Many believe that mirrors can be used as a portal by ghosts and other entities, allowing them to enter a home. Many reports have been made regarding antique mirrors connected to paranormal activity.

Richard has, in his time as a paranormal investigator, had his share of strange occurrences with mirrors. In one investigation of a family under siege by spirits, a great deal of activity had to do with an antique mirror kept in a bedroom. The first thing to happen was each time this malevolent spirit seemed to show up, there was a heavy thump from the primary bedroom. In one such instance, the homeowner—who took it upon himself to constantly carry a camera everywhere in the house—was near the bedroom when he heard this sound, and a moment he later snapped several pictures of the bedroom. One photo included the mirror, which displayed a strange scene in the reflection. Under analysis, the image in the mirror showed a woman in an old-style dress coming down an ornate staircase, two open doors with a tall man in a black suit in the doorway with his back to the scene, and a small child with a toy or doll looking up at him. Nothing like that in the primary bedroom could have produced such a reflection.

The first speculation was that the mirror was a doorway. After a few months of study, Richard found a location that matched the reflection in the mirror. The haunting was taking place in a town house that was once the servant residence for a grand mansion. When Richard entered the mansion's main floor, there it was: The same stairway and the two doors—an exact match.

How could a scene in a house a thousand yards away play itself out in a mirror in a second-floor bedroom?

Richard decided to conduct an experiment by covering the mirror with a thick black cloth in hopes of closing the hypothetical portal. The funny thing about closing doorways—as the homeowner and Richard quickly learned—is that it would be wise close a doorway when the spirit has used it to leave the house in question. In their case, it seemed they had sealed its exit. Keep this sort of thing in mind, as mirrors may be used as a doorway into your home but can also be used as an exit.

So, what is it about mirrors, specifically older mirrors, that seems so attractive to spirits? Most older mirrors have a silver-coated back to them, and silver is a very interesting metal. Silver atoms and their electrons are not densely packed. Electrons interact with light waves, which causes the electrons to move and thus the light waves to reflect. Interestingly, the electrons can match the speed of the visible and slower infrared frequencies and reflect them back. However, in the case of ultraviolet light frequencies, these light waves are much too fast and pass through the mirror. Silver, which is used in a great deal of these mirrors, has the highest electrical and thermal conductivity of any metal on the periodic table and one of the greatest levels of optical reflectivity available. It also has the lowest contact resistance of all metals.

Remember that light is an electromagnetic field and silver is electrically conductive, which will cancel the field and cause the wave to reflect away from the mirror. I have theorized for many years now that spirits have an electromagnetic field in the higher ultraviolet range of frequency. If this is the case, the conductivity of a silver-backed mirror would be attractive as a doorway, and if these spirits do operate at higher UV frequencies, they would not cancel out but rather pass through the mirror with ease.

Again, this is just a theory. Much experimentation needs to take place still.

The Spirit Box Ganzfeld Experiment (a.k.a. Estes Method)

Speaking of experimenting, it behooves us to address a growing trend in field testing, namely a variation of the Ganzfeld experiment. (See "Glossary of Paranormal Terminology.") In this television-inspired process, one team member is partially sensory-deprived by wearing noise-cancelling earphones and a blindfold (or halved Ping-Pong balls over each eye). Instead of pink-noise static, the output of a spirit box is the only sound the experimenter is subjected to via the headphones. In practice, the "blind" and "deaf" (to outside sounds) person is tasked with sharing aloud words and phrases they think they're hearing amid the cacophony of sweeping radio noise emitted by the spirit box for the benefit of the observing team members. While someone records the experiment, team members are encouraged to ask questions relevant to the research site in the hope that the sensory-deprived member, who is deaf to the line of questioning, conveys possible "replies" they're perceiving in real time.

In essence, this is a solo spirit box session that others can participate in, influenced by the experimenter's interpretations … and therein lies the problem.

By conducting this practice as described, the entire team (and its resulting conclusions) is fundamentally trusting that the spirit box listener's interpretations are accurate! With no means of hearing the spirit box output for themselves afterward, the remaining team is unable to analyze and verify the subject's perceptions. Additionally, valuable time that might have been more effectively used for gleaning pertinent field data has just been wasted.

We suggest that alternative systems of data-gathering be implemented, starting with the audio output from the spirit box. If wiring a pick-up microphone (connected to an independent audio recorder) inside one ear of the headphones is unrealistic, try incorporating an audio splitter at the source (i.e., the spirit box). One wire goes to the headphones and the other to a handheld speaker. In this manner, not only will the outside participants hear what the subject is hearing, but they will also be able to record both spirit box and interpretive outputs simultaneously. (To avoid noise contamination for future analysis, the outside participants should be advised not to speak their own interpretations of the spirit box output aloud in the moment. Instead, they should wait until analysis playback of the audio recordings of this experiment to do so.)

Going a few steps further, we would also suggest monitoring the subject themselves, using electroencephalogram (EEG), heart, and respiration rate monitors. Anecdotal evidence suggests that some people feel a temperature change preceding or during a paranormal experience—a temperature shift that does not originate externally. Certainly the monitors and devices we'd like to see implemented in this instance mean additional costs for the team, but this is the kind of science-based data that will significantly contribute to our overall understanding of paranormal study.

Communication Considerations

When trying to establish communication with a spirit, we should consider the various conditions that a spirit may be facing.

Many may not even realize they are dead. At the end of their life, they could have faced overwhelming trauma, which could cause dissociative amnesia or a complete detachment from their reality. This is a protective process where specific memories are repressed or blocked completely.

Others might remember the end event in addition to the trauma, causing them to develop post-traumatic stress disorder (PTSD), which may cause severe anxiety, anger, and flashbacks of those memories.

Those spirits that have realized their ghostly state will most likely retain their living personality indefinitely. Arguably, old habits *don't* die; ghosts can be good or bad and still hold on to the personality traits that made them who they were in life.

To establish meaningful communications, the investigator should consider all these aspects and attempt to look at situations from other points of view. Telling a spirit they are dead could result in a variety of reactions, ranging from anger to the complete shutdown of contact, negatively affecting your investigation attempts.

Provoking is rarely recommended and is only used by those who don't have the patience or skill to do things properly, in which case they should be asking themselves if they are the right person to conduct an investigation in the first place.

Know the Risks: The Problems with
Clearing a Haunted Location

There are two major issues when it comes to investigators or mediums who tell you they are going to clear your home or business of ghosts.

The first problem is they don't seem to understand the dynamics of a haunting. The majority of haunted locations rarely have one spirit. These multiple spirits, some good, some bad, maintain a balance. The balance can be off slightly, thus the reason the owner has called in a paranormal group or medium in the first place. Imagine you are out for the evening and your teenagers are having a party. You come home, walk in, shut the music off, and demand everyone leave. The first to head for the door are the polite, respectful ones who don't want any trouble. The ones who couldn't care either way depart. You are relieved, except you didn't notice that bad one hiding in the shadows brooding. The team or medium tells you job well done, and they go home. The real trouble is about to begin. The balance is gone, and this leftover bad guy has nothing to stand in his way. Your house is now his playground. Good luck trying to get those good spirits to return; it is not going to happen.

A full in-depth investigation should be done first to account for every spirit in the building and find out exactly what you are dealing with before any action is taken. Try to use conflict resolution techniques and find some common ground before you begin evicting spirits from your home or business. There is a reason it's called an investigation. There are so many factors to consider that could be causing the haunting. A true investigator will take the time to learn everything they can before making any type of decision.

The second problem is that many mediums and paranormal groups will charge money to perform a clearing. This practice is not acceptable. Good paranormal teams will never charge for their work. It's unethical. When dealing with the unknown, there are no guarantees. No one can be 100 percent sure what they are dealing with or even know for certain how many spirits may be present—let alone be aware of their intentions. We have seen the result of several well-meaning rituals that have made situations worse, and nothing that has worked 100 percent.

When looking for someone to help you with a paranormal situation, ask for references; see how they handled previous cases. Find out what options they suggest and be sure they are committed to staying on the job until it is resolved to the best of their ability.

Smoke Cleansing

The original intention behind the ritual of smoke cleansing to clear negative energies from participants and the environment has become confused in popular culture and beliefs. The term *smudging* has been appropriated from Indigenous cultures and has unfortunately become ingrained in the New Age and paranormal zeitgeist.

The original targets of smoke cleansing were unpleasant energies considered harmful in the sense of negativity, anxieties, depression, bad thoughts, dark moods/emotions, or even sickness. This ritual provided a balanced environment of peace and harmony and was not originally designed or intended to displace human or nonhuman entities.

After studying hundreds of cases where smoke cleansing was used to clear a spirit, a remarkable pattern emerged. In 97 percent of cases, the activity in the dwelling ceased for three days on average before returning with an even stronger intensity than before, with a more destructive focus toward the living.

Chapter 2
TEAMS

S hould you wish to be part of a team, we recommend searching online or through community word of mouth for organizations operating in your area. Do your research. For example, learn the types of locations they visit. Is their method of work or level of seriousness of interest to you? Are they currently active? Do they seem reputable and follow the law? Can they provide references? If you feel there are aspects about this team that appeal to you, make contact and inquire whether they are interested in taking on a new member—one who has studied this very manual!

Assembling a Team

The journey before you is fraught with many highlights and letdowns, including new discoveries when you least expect them and confirmation of experiences that others have already reported worldwide. Failure to capture evidence is not a reflection of you and your devotion to learning more and advancing the study of ghost phenomena. Deducing methods that *don't* work is just as important.

Keeping this in mind, it's up to you to assemble a team of likeminded searchers—people who not only share the passion but are willing to do the work involved to the best of their abilities.

If you're a team leader, you'll be dealing with a mix of egos, emotions, and ideas concerning what it means to behave as a professional paranormal investigator. Use this manual as your touchstone and share it with potential members. The truly dedicated will appreciate and respect your honest purpose, and the thrill-seekers will withdraw.

If you're a member of a team and wish to apply your abilities to better the reputation of your group and further your collective learning experience delving firsthand into ghost phenomena, use this manual as your touchstone, too. If every member is on the same page while they contribute their specialized abilities on and off the field, consider what can be accomplished.

Code, Ethics, and Integrity: Protecting Yourself and Your Clients

Ethics is one of the most important attributes a team will have. It will command everything you do, how you do it, and how you act, react, and behave. It will determine how honest and responsible you are. By observing your ethical practices, clients and property owners will develop respect for you and your team, and this can lead to other investigative jobs.

When assembling a team, it is absolutely imperative that every member understands and agrees to adhere to a strict code of ethics and integrity before they are permitted to participate in the field. Every person, including guests, should always act in a professional manner, maintain safe work practices, never knowingly place themselves or others in harm's way, act in the best interest of all people living or dead, and respect individual, cultural, and role differences.

Imagine you are the client reaching out for assistance, perhaps being wary of agreeing to allow a team to investigate your property.

Whether they admit it or not, your clients are in a vulnerable position as they open their private world to a team of complete strangers that bring with them field expertise, willingness to help, and their own individual biases and judgments regarding the task at hand.

As a team leader, it is your responsibility to be observant of your members' performance and to assure your clients that their trust in your team and its capabilities is sound and justified. Do so on a consistent basis.

Leave It As You Found It

When the investigation has concluded and it's time to pack your gear and exit, make sure the location is in the same state it was in when you first entered. Dispose of refuse, return items that were moved in the course of your visit to where they were originally positioned, and clean up any messes before leaving.

The Searcher Group has made it a practice to bring garbage and recycling bags to each worksite to take team refuse away with us completely. As eccentric and unnecessary as this may seem to you (or your clients), doing so is a simple, unexpected, and memorable deed that reflects advantageously on the team long after it has left the property. Your clients will appreciate this show of respect and care for their property. This finishing touch may influence their decision to grant you return access at a later date.

Personal Behavior

The prospect of beginning an investigation is exciting. It's important that each member displays energy and enthusiasm for the job ahead, but it is absolutely imperative that everyone demonstrates a professional focus and restraint.

Respect the wishes of the clients at all times, which can range from removing shoes at the front door to avoiding areas they expressly forbid accessing. Though it seems silly to broach, asking if it is okay to access a client's restroom is encouraged. This degree of politeness will aid in establishing your clients' comfort level as they observe your team at work.

While the clients will likely address most questions and concerns to the team leader, know that if they opt to participate in the investigation, they will likely interact with all team members at various times. Before arriving on site, remind your teammates to conduct themselves respectfully and encourage them to not only listen to the client but to ask and log relevant questions pertaining to the activity they are perceiving.

When interacting with your client, you may be tempted to share your own experiences from other field cases. Do your best to keep your comments brief and save the details of your personal stories for rest periods outside the investigation site. As team leader, advise your clients of this practice at the onset so the team members won't come across as rude in the clients' eyes if their replies are too succinct.

Follow the Leader

If you're a team leader, adopt an informal protocol with the team members. Discuss it beforehand, but remind them as soon as they arrive on site that they should:

- refrain from speaking all at once or out of turn;
- "tag" their activities and movements aloud for the benefit of audio recorders (whispering, grunts, stomach gurgles, and so on) to help distinguish sounds made by team members from something unidentifiable or even paranormal;

- "tag" noises that are native to the investigation site (e.g., HVAC, sump pump, air freshener activation, exterior traffic, and so on);
- conduct their experimentation where directed;
- inform you of their whereabouts at all times;
- refrain from blurting sensational statements in front of the client (e.g., "That shadow reminded me of a demon!"); and
- never swear or use derogatory language at any time.

Once at the investigation location, clear-cut organization is key. When any audio or video recording equipment has been activated, all conversations between team members should be minimal. You are there to record the environment and how unseen entities react to your presence, not each other.

In cases where audio recording gear outnumbers video recorders, team members should clearly identify themselves and mark the time of day aloud when they enter and exit rooms. Doing so will aid in reconstructing a timeline of events in the final report and help debunk questionable sounds detected by investigators in one area that were actually created by other members of the team located elsewhere.

Monitoring Personal Emotions

If you are the team leader, establish protocol with your team regarding what to do in the event of extreme, unexpected circumstances, such as when a team member or guest of the team is suddenly attacked or injured by an unseen force.

In this situation, immediately come to the victim's aid and administer care to ensure their health and well-being. See that the injured person recovers, and escort them outside the investigation site if necessary.

Once the victim receives treatment, a secondary instinct may be to antagonize the ghostly assailant. While outright assaults have been far and few between in our experience, when they have happened, we have witnessed investigators shout their irate objections to the empty air and try to provoke a secondary attack that can be documented by the team's equipment as a form of negative communication. Though you may feel that the team is at the mercy of an invisible aggressor who is deliberately cajoling you, trying to push your collective buttons, remember that you are *not* there to engage in a fight you cannot possibly win. Unfortunately, we have experienced instances like this— with clients in attendance—and the resulting level of discomfort always weighs heavily for everyone involved for the remainder of the investigation.

We recommend that your team addresses this eventuality, discussing how its members might react so they can develop a strategy on how to deal with such situations. Use this time to establish how individual members who express themselves more intensely than others can be diffused by the more composed team members during a heated situation.

Management and Development of Teams

The excitement of venturing out to conduct a paranormal investigation can be enormous. The idea of exploring a reputedly haunted location with the possibility of capturing evidence is thrilling. Whether you are part of a team or like to explore on your own, safety must always remain on your mind as the number one priority.

Doing this type of work alone is not recommended. That being said, people do work alone for their own reasons. We can understand that when alone, an investigator doesn't have to worry about outsider audio contamination or trying to decide who is going to do what job. The main problem is if—or when—something goes wrong, you will have no one readily available to help you. If investigating solo, you should have an emergency plan, and people you trust should know where you are going and what time you will come home. It is important to stick to these arrangements.

Even small teams must use extreme caution, especially when investigating old buildings. Working closely, along with the excitement of the investigation, could mean everyone ends up in the same space at the same time. A team Richard worked with years ago entered a large underground basement. The place was in terrible repair, and the steel fire door they entered through somehow closed behind them. The investigators found they were trapped inside heavy concrete and steel construction with no cellular phone service available. Luckily, a security guard found them—hours later. We need to keep these things in mind when on an investigation.

The workload is heavier with a small team, as many tasks need to be carried out by fewer people. Investigators are tasked with managing longer lists of details to focus on, which could reduce valuable time available to conduct thorough investigative work. For example, let's say a small team has been permitted to conduct an eight-hour investigation. Two of those hours will be spent setting and packing up the equipment, which leaves six hours to investigate. With larger teams, the investigators can investigate for the full eight hours while other members set up and tear down equipment.

It is great if you can put a team together comprised of people you already know and trust; however, because of the special skills required, you may have to recruit strangers. When doing so, check into their background and do extensive interviews. Try to be satisfied with the information and answers you receive. Be absolutely sure these people will represent you and the group faithfully and be responsible when handling equipment, collecting information, and respecting the investigation site—including keeping it confidential.

Team Assignments

Every team will be different. Some will have set roles and duties, while others mix it up by changing roles and duties for team members so they gain different training and experience. It doesn't matter which route you take. Neither one is better than the other. It is all about preference and what works best for the team. However, when working a location for numerous visits, team members should maintain their original roles throughout the ongoing investigation to be consistent. Traditional team member roles include the following:

Lead Investigator

The job of the lead investigator is to form the plan for each investigation or visit, assign jobs to the other team members, and ensure everyone is doing their assignments. They also make sure evidence is properly collected and everyone conducts themselves safely.

Investigator

An investigator conducts tests and experiments and records electronic voice phenomena during the investigation. Investigators should conduct walk throughs of the study site prior to the investigation to collect baseline readings, become familiar with the layout, and make sure it's safe, noting any dangerous areas.

At least one of the investigators should have a good working knowledge on interviewing witnesses, including how to make a witness feel at ease, what questions to ask, and how to collect and record the information. (See "Interviewing Witnesses" in chapter 4.)

Tech

The tech team members make sure all the surveillance equipment is deployed in locations indicated by the lead investigator, ensuring optimal camera views. The tech team members verify all camera and audio equipment is working, that camera views are the best they can be, and that sound levels are optimized. Additionally, they ensure fresh batteries are available for mobile equipment, provide technical support and information when requested, and perform analysis of recorded data following the investigation.

Researcher/Historian

This team member is responsible for collecting detailed historical information about the property and the past owners, along with any relevant events in the property's history. They can also assist in investigations.

Mediums

Finding the right medium(s) for your team is key and can be extremely difficult. Many mediums are hoaxers, fakes, or attention-seekers looking to augment their social status. Some of the most committed, helpful mediums are those with a humble attitude toward their gifts; they recognize their worth in this context as a human tool connected to an investigation and don't expect praise over and above the team's appreciation for their contribution. Legitimately talented psychic mediums can operate on a spectrum from fairly good to mostly accurate to exceptional. Truly capable mediums will not fish for information connected to an investigation and will insist that they discover what they can for themselves. Recruiting the right one could take time.

As if recruiting a good one isn't difficult enough, you must find the *right* type, which is even more of a challenge.

Psychic or mental medium: This type of medium communicates through the use of telepathy, which allows the medium to hear, see, and feel information from spirits.

Trance medium: This type of medium enters a trance state, allowing spirits to communicate through them. While in a trance, the medium will rarely remember any of the message, so it is important to record what they are saying.

Physical medium: This type of medium utilizes a variety of means to establish inter-dimensional communication. Methods can be visual (manifestations, apport objects) or audible (raps, knocks, disembodied voices) in nature. In some cases, both visual and audible events occur.

Some terminology of the mechanisms employed by mediums:

Clairaudience, or "clear hearing": This the ability to hear the voices or thoughts broadcast by spirits.

Clairvoyance, or "clear seeing": This is the ability to see things that are not physically evident.

Clairsentience, or "clear sensing": This is the ability to sense information that a spirit wishes to communicate.

Clairalience, or "clear smelling": This is the ability to smell a spirit or thing directly associated with a spirit, such as perfume or cigar smoke.

Clairgustance, or "clear tasting": This is the ability, albeit rare, to taste impressions from a spirit.

Claircognizance, or "clear knowing": This is the ability to simply know something. It is the ability to tell if some information is right or wrong, true or false.

Empaths: Being empathic means a medium has the ability to understand feelings and experiences that are not their own but conveyed to them. An empath may take on the feelings of the spirit, such as anger, frustration, sadness, depression, or pain, for a short while.

Mediums should never know anything about the location, the history of the property, or any discoveries made in the course of your research or investigation.

Safety and Security (S&S) Specialist

S&S specialists are those who observe the team from a distance for the purposes of safety and security. They maintain their distance so if something goes wrong, they are not directly involved or endangered (e.g., injured or trapped) and are free to provide assistance. (As an example, recall the previous anecdote concerning the lack of cell phone service while locked inside a concrete room located deep underground.)

Finding Professional Support

Paranormal investigation groups are usually familiar with other groups in the area, country, or world. It is wise to become familiar with these other groups and study their ethics and ability to help those in need. A reputable group should demonstrate good ethics, have the resources to provide assistance, and be willing to work within a network of professionals. Connect with them, open a line of communication, and form a mutual agreement to share information and assist those in need.

All too often a case will come to your attention via email, on social media, or through your website that proves impossible to logistically respond to. By building a professional association, you will be able to refer the person requesting help to a team working in their vicinity.

When a group refers a case to another team, the referring group should be kept in the loop as to what is being done to assist the client and any conclusion or results made. This allows those requesting assistance to receive the care and concern they require.

Clients and Team Conduct

Whether the job has surfaced as a call for help or from a location you've taken steps to inquire about, every property owner, committee member, and site manager is considered a client. First impressions are key. Exude warmth and friendliness when introducing yourself, describe your role on the team, and share the code of conduct that every member will follow on the job.

Never infringe or violate the trust of a client, and always hold the client's privacy and property as the highest priority. Names, events, property locations, and other information regarding cases should never appear in print or online, nor be discussed in a public forum without express written permission from the client. In the unlikely event your team encounters legal trouble over confidentiality issues, you'll have documented proof of authorization.

Always be completely honest with your client. Keep appropriate records and maintain a mutually agreed-upon briefing with them regarding the work, its progress, and any challenges encountered. Never falsify information or omit data when briefing the client.

Be sensitive to delicate information regarding the client or other people you discover during research and investigations. Consider potential harm and the feelings of living people, especially if delicate information pertaining to your investigation is released. For example, during a case Richard worked, the team uncovered ninety-eight-year-old evidence of childhood sexual abuse; the client family requested that this information not be shared in a public forum. Sometimes understanding, trust, and ethics trump the story being told.

Fully understand the limits of your personal knowledge regarding the paranormal. Limit your conclusions and resolutions made to the client to that framework of knowledge. Do not jump to unfounded conclusions or provide far-fetched theories that may exacerbate the situation the client is already facing.

Never charge money for an investigation. You and your team are offering to scrutinize your client's claims, looking for naturally occurring phenomena to explain questionable occurrences or to validate a paranormal manifestation and express opinions on how to resolve the situation. To charge money for this service would be to declare you have the appropriate knowledge of the issue and the ability to correct this situation to the client's satisfaction. This means you are legally liable for anything that goes wrong, including the dissatisfaction of the client. Furthermore, once you charge money for your service, you could be charged with fraud should the client feel you are not handling their situation to their satisfaction, and they could levy charges against you with the authorities. Very specific laws exist and vary widely from location to location. For example, a fortune-teller in California has the right to predict the future, but in New York State, fortune-telling is a Class B misdemeanor and can carry a five-hundred-dollar fine. This includes services that exorcise curses or manipulate paranormal events. In one case, the perpetrator extended the duration of their services, demanded more money, and was ultimately convicted of grand larceny and fraud and sentenced to fifteen years in a state prison. In England and Wales, there's the Fraudulent Mediums Act of 1951, and the five cases that were tried between 1980 and 1995 all resulted in convictions.

Prior to committing to a paranormal case, establish a clear understanding of when either party may terminate any further activity, action, or agreement. This event may occur for several reasons, and the client can do so for any number of reasons at any time, without warning or explanation. However, should you or your team decide to conclude the work without completion or resolution because of logistical reasons, because you feel the investigation is faltering, or due to lack of resources, be prepared to provide a referral or a replacement team to fulfill the original commitment should the client desire proper closure to the case.

The Power of Membership

There are many professional educational and research centers located around the globe, and a few are listed in the following sections. These institutions can provide even the most seasoned investigator with current research, theories, and other resources such as peer review and professional guidance. Any serious investigator should belong to a network of professional associations.

> **The Ghost Club** is reputed to be the world's oldest paranormal investigation and research organization. Its roots extend back to Cambridge, England, in 1855, but it officially launched in London in 1862. Its membership boasts several notable names, including author Charles Dickens, investigator Harry Price, actor Peter Cushing, and author and parapsychologist Peter Underwood. Though a not-for-profit organization, membership (as of this writing) starts at twenty-five pounds for one person and thirty-five pounds for two at once. Members today receive quarterly digital journals and access to organized investigations. Learn more at www.ghostclub.org.uk.

The Society for Psychical Research (SPR) was founded in England in 1882. Its website declares that the SPR is "the first organisation to conduct scholarly research into human experiences that challenge contemporary scientific models."[11] Indeed, the SPR founders included academically minded figures such as philosophy professor Henry Sidgwick, classical scholar Frederic Myers, psychologist Edmund Gurney, and physicists William Barrett and Lord Rayleigh. As of this writing, regular annual membership is eighty-four pounds; however, its mailing list is free to join if you wish to receive SPR updates. Learn more at www.spr.ac.uk/home.

The Rhine Research Center is an independent, nonprofit parapsychology research center that originated in 1928 at Duke University in Durham, North Carolina. Named for pioneering researcher Joseph B. Rhine, the RRC continues to "produce original research and explore the nature of human consciousness," according to its website.[12] As of this writing, there are eight membership options, starting at ten dollars for monthly access to online archives, meetings, and past events. Learn more at www.rhineonline.org.

The Koestler Parapsychology Unit is located at the University of Edinburgh, Scotland. Founded in 1962, the Koestler Parapsychology Unit continues to conduct research into psi, paranormal belief systems, and the history of accounts of anomalous phenomena. Learn more at www.ed .ac.uk/ppls/psychology/prospective/postgraduate/research -programmes/research-interests/parapsychology.

. . . .

11. "Society for Psychical Research."
12. "What Is the Rhine?"

The American Society for Psychical Research (ASPR) was founded in 1885 as a North American offshoot of England's SPR and pioneered by representatives in the fields of physics, psychiatry, psychology, and even astronomy. There are five options for one interested in joining, starting at seventy dollars as of this writing. Learn more at www.aspr.com.

The Institute of Noetic Sciences (IONS) was founded by Apollo 14 astronaut Dr. Edgar Mitchell in 1973 after "a profound experience of personal discovery." The IONS website explains that multidisciplinary scientists conduct "research on frontier topics in consciousness and its impact on our lives."[13] Learn more at www.noetic.org.

The Parapsychology Foundation was founded in 1951 and supports scientific investigation of psychic phenomena. Based in New York City, the Parapsychology Foundation also provides resource materials to academic and lay communities. Programs and publication access are available by submitting your email address. Learn more at parapsychology.org.

....
13. "Institute of Noetic Sciences (IONS)."

Chapter 3
EQUIPMENT AND TOOLS

Contrary to the assumptions fans of paranormal reality TV make, there is nothing in the industry that is designed specifically for the investigation of spirits. It is important to understand the types of equipment you use, how they are used, what the operating parameters are, what they were specifically designed to do, and just how they apply to what you are using them for.

You are not using equipment to hunt ghosts. You are using equipment to assess the environment, seek anomalies within the surroundings, and try to determine why those anomalies exist. Even then, the only way to detect abnormalities is to conduct and log multiple baseline measurements over many areas over a lengthy period of time.

The development of digital data storage systems, including secure digital (SD) cards, hard drives, and digital video recorders (DVRs), has made the investigator's equipment lighter, less expensive, and easier to store. However, newer technology can also work against us in paranormal investigation. Analog systems were very difficult to hoax or doctor. Photographic film produced a negative, and VHS and cassette tape systems could easily be checked for indications of tampering. These analog and physical media systems produced the best undisputed evidence, but the resulting quality left much to be desired.

Unfortunately, digital systems (audio and video) can be easily manipulated and altered. Even today, most digital evidence is rarely admissible in court. (See "Analyzing Photos and Video" in chapter 6 for a solution to the issue of evidence manipulation.)

Another problem is what is known as the *CSI* effect. You might capture some great evidence, but the overall quality might be fuzzy. Once we start to augment a digital image by enhancing brightness, contrasts, and colors and removing video noise and graininess, the end result may spark an argument that the image offered has been so greatly altered that it no longer represents an accurate portrayal of the original.

Keeping all this in mind, let's delve into field equipment, including high tech, low tech, and outside-the-box suggestions your team may be inspired to try.

Environment-Measuring Equipment

If most of the world's teams purporting to call themselves "paranormal investigators" were asked to be honest and name the most appealing aspect related to the task, odds are the chance to utilize electronic equipment that alarms at the slightest environmental changes would be their top incentive. Trusting the sensations our own bodies register while walking around a deserted asylum or prison doesn't quite compare to the unmistakable thrill of flashing lights and shrill beeping sounds suddenly erupting from an expensive science-based detection device.

Regardless of the excitement that comes with tangible detection of anomalous spikes in energy while exploring in the field, a truly professional investigator must accept a basic truth: Despite the marketing ploys of some clever manufacturers, none of the devices discussed here qualifies as a ghost detector on its own.

What needs to be understood is that each of these instruments performs for the purpose it was originally designed for: To alert the user to changes in the environment. Period.

As professional investigators, it is up to us to note and compare environmental changes as they happen in the course of an investigation and corroborate them with other occurrences (physical, visual, or audible) before assuming we are in the presence of a ghost, let alone presume we are communicating with one.

Let's review environmental factors an investigator needs to monitor and the tools of other trades that have been adopted for use in ours.

Electromagnetic Field Meters

Prior to the reality TV craze of the early 2000s, EMF-detecting devices were utilized solely by electricians, property developers, home inspectors, and other industries that log electromagnetic field measurements as part of their respective duties. Once EMF meters began appearing on *Most Haunted* and *Ghost Hunters*, the paranormal investigation field—and the researcher's tool kit—changed forever.

EMF meters measure fluctuations in electromagnetic fields. The units of measurement registered on an EMF meter are called milligauss (mG). There are two main types of EMF meters: Single-axis and tri-field (or tri-axis) meters.

Single-axis EMF meters measure fluctuations in electromagnetic fields in only one direction, which will be directly in front of you.

Tri-field meters measure fluctuations in electromagnetic fields on three axis points: X, Y, and Z. These devices measure in all directions.

Having a variety of EMF-detecting meters handy in the field is an excellent idea, and we recommend becoming acquainted with single-axis EMF meters as well as tri-field meters that detect naturally produced electromagnetic energy. Most of these meters have a limited effective range of about ten feet, and you should consult your owner's manual for details.

As much as a spike in EMF energy may signal the presence of a ghost, it is also possible that you may someday witness an unmistakable manifestation while there is a *lack* of a detectable energy flux. Either way, you and your team will never be able to scientifically log that aspect of the environment without an EMF meter present, so continuously use them and log the results accurately for future reference.

Prices for EMF meters vary according to their respective abilities. Unsurprisingly, the prevalence of these devices on numerous television shows helped boost sales and inspired some to market them directly to eager ghost hunters in the name of fun and entertainment.

If an EMF meter isn't available, or if its battery power has been unexpectedly drained, a compass can be used to detect the presence of magnetic fluctuations. The Searcher Group has experienced a number of instances when a compass needle could not find magnetic north and would spin erratically while resting on a flat surface but would operate normally once it was moved a few feet away. To ensure the instrument was not malfunctioning, it was returned to the areas where odd readings occurred previously, but now showed that the magnetic anomaly had moved elsewhere or was completely absent.

Hygrometers

Since water movement produces electricity, which may be used by a spirit to manifest in any number of ways, incorporating a hygrometer to measure and log changes in the humidity present at an investigation site is recommended. Some digital thermometers include hygrometers as a secondary function. Among the physical sensations people who have experienced paranormal phenomena report feeling relates to static charges in the environment.

Electrostatic Field Meters

While arguably goose bumps and body hair standing on end can be explained physiologically as a response to fright, it's ideal to incorporate an electrostatic field meter when logging the environmental data at a jobsite. Have a team member keep this device handy during subsequent walk throughs and note inconsistencies—especially in the event an unexplained occurrence takes place while investigating!

Ion Counters

In cases where you've been called upon to help a client, using an ion counter to note the number of negative/good to positive/bad ions in the air will be useful in terms of finding a normal explanation for claims of anxiety, fatigue, headaches, and nausea. We investigate to rule out the many natural possibilities for a client's issue before we can assume something supernatural is behind it. Ultimately, you may find yourself recommending they invest in an air ionizer instead of a spiritual clearing.

Thermometers

Logging temperature fluctuations of the investigation site throughout the course of your investigation is an absolute must, and a thermometer is likely the least expensive piece of gear you'll find on this list. There are digital infrared laser thermometers available to take measurements from a distance, but when we're in the business of noting environmental changes when it comes to ghosts, a basic thermometer is all that should be included in your kit.

Geophones

Since footfalls, raps, taps, knocks, and objects colliding with each other create vibrations, a geophone has become a necessary (but expensive) piece of equipment. While it's possible to assemble one yourself, a geophone is included as a function of the EDI+ Meter (along with EMF, air pressure, temperature, and humidity-measuring capabilities), assuming the three-hundred-dollar (Canadian) retail price doesn't dissuade you from owning one or two.

Geiger Counters

While radiation is not normally associated with ghosts themselves, it *is* related to alleged dimensional portals. In the event your team measures abnormally high EMF fluctuations where none should be— or if your reliable psychic medium pinpoints a location purporting to be a portal—having a Geiger counter ready to confirm or debunk an indication of radiation will only help serve our collective research cause.

Additional Notes

For in-depth scientific information regarding environmental factors connected with haunted locations, read the excellent study "Things That Go Bump in the Literature: An Environmental Appraisal of 'Haunted Houses.'" (See "Resources.")

Remember to remove the batteries from your equipment after an investigation. Too often batteries leak, corroding the device's terminals and resulting in irreparable damage to valuable equipment.

Video Cameras

A basic tool of any investigation is a video camera. It serves two purposes: To attempt to capture paranormal activity and to document your investigation.

There are two main types of video cameras. The first is the handheld mobile system, such as a camcorder. These are carried around to film action in real time. The second type is surveillance cameras. These are fixed in a location to monitor a specific area or object. Surveillance cameras include closed-circuit television (CCTV) or an open system. A CCTV system is local, meaning the entire system is contained on location and the signal from the cameras used is sent to a monitor and recording medium, typically a DVR located in the same general area. An open system sends the camera data to an IP network with a network video recorder (NVR), allowing the video information to be viewed remotely. The major difference is that an NVR system can be viewed anywhere in the world while a DVR system is limited to the length of wire connecting the camera to the recording system.

Camcorders and other standalone cameras can be used as surveillance cameras when placed in a fixed location. However, these cameras record to an insertable flash memory or SD memory card, which are extremely limited in terms of data storage and cannot be monitored in real time.

It is crucial to remove data-filled SD cards from your camera devices and secure them to preserve evidence and metadata. Making digital copies to enhance and analyze is fine, but the raw, unaltered data must be preserved. (See "Analyzing Photos and Video" in chapter 6.)

Whether using mobile cameras or surveillance cameras, it is best to use camera systems with add-on or built-in audio microphones. This will allow the collection and capture of all available visual and auditory information within your target areas.

Before deploying cameras, the investigator should consider all available information collected from eyewitness accounts and baseline readings to determine the best camera placement to document the most promising locations; ideally, you want the best views to monitor the largest areas possible. A camera mounted in a corner that captures footpaths, doorways, mirrors, and parts of other rooms from a high-angle vantage point is recommended.

Depending on the size of the location you are investigating, it will most likely be impossible to see everything, so camera placement is key. Remember that the more cameras used, the more data review required afterward. For example, if four cameras are used during an eight-hour investigation, this means thirty-two hours of data will need to be scrutinized. In reality, because of the start-stop, rewind-and-playback nature of the review process, you're likely looking at thirty-six hours of analysis time or more, as some data may require closer sifting more than once. There are no shortcuts; this is the reality of true paranormal investigation.

Areas under surveillance should be marked, or at a minimum, the team should be fully aware of the locations. When entering these areas, a team member should simply state their name and the time, conduct their business (being mindful not to block the view of the camera), and upon leaving, again state their name and the time of their exit.

When using video cameras to monitor doors that have been reported to open by themselves, remember that in most cases the hardware will not translate well on video recordings, meaning the door may open but the viewer will probably not be able to tell if the door handle itself moved. Affix a small, bright piece of paper to the handle or dab a simple dot of Wite-Out on it to give the viewer a point of reference for the handle's orientation at rest. Should the handle move, the action will be obvious during analysis later.

In some situations, cameras can be tampered with by unseen forces, either by being moved, shut off, or knocked over. In these situations, it would be wise to use a cross-surveillance technique where one camera watches another and vice versa. Should one camera be involved in an incident, the other camera might capture the event.

Ideally, cameras should be placed as close to a wall or solid structure as possible, and entry and exit points ought to be in view.

If your cameras can be hidden or disguised, deploy them covertly where possible. While some ghosts will likely observe the set-up procedure, aware of the purpose of cameras and making a conscious effort to avoid them, others may arrive or manifest at the location at a later hour, ignorant of the cameras' presence. Use your imagination regarding this practice; just be careful not to cause a camera system to overheat.

Some professional-grade surveillance systems will have a camera control panel that can provide several functions for cameras that are equipped with servomotors. These cameras are called PTZs (pan-tilt-zoom), as they're able to pan (move back and forth horizontally), tilt (move up and down), and zoom in to examine areas and objects closely. Some also provide an automatic tracking system. These cameras have motion detectors built into them, allowing the cameras to automatically follow activity.

Within the visual light spectrum, which is a segment of the electromagnetic spectrum, the human eye can detect wavelengths of 380 to 700 nanometers (nm). With specific filters removed, a camera lens is able to see beyond the visible light spectrum and into the infrared spectrum (760 to 1000 nm), the ultraviolet spectrum (315 to 400 nm), or both. A camera designed to look at the visible spectrum while extending our view into both IR and UV is commonly known as a full-spectrum camera.

Ultraviolet: Approximately 280–380 nm

Standard daylight (visible light): Approximately 380–760 nm

Infrared night vision: Approximately 760–900 nm

Full spectrum: Approximately 300–850 nm

Thermal imaging: Approximately 1000–14,000 nm

When using a modified camera to see into IR, UV, or full spectrum, you will be required to use special lighting to illuminate what the camera can see and to maximize the clearest captured image possible. Ghost equipment dealers often carry a variety of IR and UV light illumination devices that are specifically designed to supplement still and video camera systems, in order to "see" farther than the abilities built into the camera. Investing in tripod mount brackets to attach two or more devices at once is recommended.

Instrumental transcommunication (ITC) is a technique designed by German-born Klaus Schreiber (1925–1988) in the 1980s. The method involves a video loop, where a video camera is set up facing a TV or monitor that displays the output from the video camera. It is an interesting technique with fairly good results in capturing images of people, animals, scenery, and even extraterrestrials and interdimensional entities that are not otherwise displayed.[14]

The method calls for setting the focal point of the camera just beyond the monitor, making the image on the monitor slightly out of focus or slightly blurry. The observer should notice an image that appears to resemble swirling clouds on the monitor screen.

Once the camera is set to record, the investigator should conduct an EVP session and ask questions. It would be wise to keep these

. . . .

14. Garrigue and Lecot, "A Note about Reproducibility in Visual ITC."

sessions short, as under later review of the recording, every single frame must be examined.

Other Equipment to Consider

The following equipment can assist in detecting phenomena and help to track trends associated with ghosts and hauntings, which could lead to building theory.

UV Meter

A UV meter detects fluctuations in ultraviolet radiation. Spirits have been recorded producing ultraviolet light. Detecting this light in places where it should not occur could be very important to your investigation.

Static Field Meter

Ghosts can create static electricity, and a static field meter is very helpful in detecting low sounds that might go unnoticed. Frequency counters have been found to detect extremely low frequencies where they should not exist. They have discovered 4 hertz (Hz) reading in areas without any reasonable explanation.

Parabolic Microphone

A parabolic microphone detects sound frequencies outside the human hearing range and amplifies them accordingly. Parabolic microphones are portable, can be mounted to tripods, and can be connected to digital recorders. This device works very well, especially if you can acquire a digital recorder that can detect sounds between the 15 and 10 Hz range.

Door Alarms

Door alarms will notify you if a door has been opened within the investigation area. These units comprise a pair of magnetic sensors that form a connection when the door is closed and sound an audible alarm when that connection is broken. They are a relatively inexpensive way to keep track of interior, exterior, and closet doors while working in a building. Installation is simple. They're positioned in place with double-sided tape and can be added and removed without causing damage.

Advanced Technology

The following tools can be very expensive, but they can be utilized for specific details within an investigation.

Drones are great for getting a literal overview of the property you are working on. You can mark out locations where exterior activity has been reported and may discover hidden or missed areas of interest on larger properties. Be sure to consult local privacy laws and drone ordinance use, and always respect the privacy of the neighbors.

Ground-penetrating radar is excellent for searching out hidden tunnels, underground chambers, and unmarked graves. If any human remains are discovered, you must immediately stop, protect the area, and report it to the local authorities. Never remove anything from a place human remains have been discovered, as you could face criminal charges.

Voice Recording Equipment

Over the years we have experimented with both analog and digital devices for capturing electronic voice phenomena. In our opinion, analog is better overall.

In several experiments, we used both digital and analog recording devices side by side at various haunted locations and found more EVP captured on the analog devices.

While analog has good reasons to be superior, there are, of course, pros and cons to both types of systems.

Scientists have studied and written extensively on why people seem to respond emotionally to recorded music, especially if the recording is analog. Although the mystery remains, one thing discovered was that analog recordings produce sound waves that are smooth and continuous, whereas digital recordings provide a sequence of square waves that build a harmonic barrier between the music and the listener. This could simply be because digitally produced sound is foreign to the human anatomy, as the human ear is physically built for analog.

Digital recordings have limited bandwidth, whereas analog is unlimited and can gain higher resolutions without loss of quality. Analog recordings will capture all frequencies and will record them exactly. Digital will only approximate these frequencies.

Digital recordings, however, will not degrade over time, whereas analog recordings will eventually suffer high frequency loss, and they are prone to errors.

Electronic Voice Phenomena

Before we discuss EVPs, the closest item to "real science" ghost investigators can share with the world, let's discuss the primary means of attaining our results, namely, white and pink noise.

> *White noise:* Also referred to as broadband noise, white noise contains all frequencies found in the spectrum of sounds the human ear can perceive, in equal parts. Paranormal

researchers believe white noise provides an easy conduit for the dead to communicate through due to the wide range of frequencies within it.

Pink noise: Also referred to as ambient noise, pink noise is similar to white noise but with lower sound waves and a lower pitch; basically, it is used to help filter out background sounds, such as people talking or cars passing by. Very little experimentation has been done with pink noise, and the current studies of the use of pink noise as a viable carrier wave for spirit communication are inconclusive.

Since the first "phantom" utterances were allegedly captured by Attila von Szalay (1909–1999) in 1941, electronic voice phenomena has become the most valued evidence pointing to the truth of the existence of life after life for investigators and researchers worldwide.

In EVPs, discarnate voices are actually responding to the investigator's presence, answering their questions directly; they are even captured conversing with each other when no one "of the flesh" is present. When we eliminate skeptics' assertions that every recorded EVP is either a stray radio signal or a misinterpreted natural sound, we are left with a significant development indeed.

Just as there are varying degrees of visual and physical manifestations by ghosts, EVPs also run the range in intensity, from sounding incredibly faint and distant to resonating as loudly and concretely as anyone physically near the microphone or recording device would sound.

Not to be mistaken for disembodied voices (DV), which are heard in real time by the naked ear, EVPs have been captured in empty, environmentally controlled spaces, as well as recorded interjecting between the voices of conversing investigators.

Our critics try to entrap us by asking, "If a dead person no longer has access to vocal cords, how is it they are able to speak as clearly as a living person?" These same closed-minded pundits usually don't stay around to hear the simple answer: Spirit people not only retain emotions and memories of their physical existence but also remember how to speak and what they sounded like!

The ability to pierce the frequencies that separate the "living" from the "dead" in order to communicate is a serious and significant hurdle to overcome, and rare is the spirit person with the capability to be heard through the naked ear by someone existing in the physical. Enter audio-recording technology, complete with microphones adept at sensing (and subsequently boosting) sound waves that ride on frequencies far too low for the average human ear to register in the moment they are broadcast.

Hoarse Whisperers: Varieties of EVP

As we explain to laypeople interested in our work, spirit voices don't normally sound like yours and ours. We must appreciate that articulated sounds must take a great deal of effort and energy to transmit between a spirit's plane and ours—especially as they lack a physical vocal apparatus.

So, until mainstream science takes the word of a genuinely gifted medium at face value, our recording equipment is the primary and most reliable choice of device when it comes to logging voices unheard by the naked ear.

When The Searcher Group trains new members in the field, Paul advises each participant on what they should be listening for, both on site (while using a parabolic microphone, for example) and when analyzing their recorded data post-investigation. Paul has coined the term *hushed whisper* to describe the majority of disembodied vocal intonations our team has been fortunate to capture, but we have recorded other varieties and intensities, too, including shouts, inter-spirit instructions, taunting, demands, pleas, critiques, insults, candid comments, humor, and pleasant, direct answers, just to name a few.

Your team may also record disembodied animal noises; between our cameras and recorders, we've captured the sounds of cats, dogs, and even the distinctive exhale of a horse!

The quantity and quality of EVP recordings will vary by location. As spirit people must draw energy from somewhere in order to assist their communication efforts, you may find you receive more responses in places located close to running water (e.g., indoor plumbing, underground streams, fountains, creeks, rivers, and lakes), hydro towers, heat sources, and dry, static-prone areas.

Research-Advancing EVP

One of our most thought-provoking EVP captures was not the result of a Q and A session at all but instead recorded by a surveillance camera in the parlor of a former Victorian-era farmhouse at approximately ten at night. The audio was of an unseen woman prompting in an affectionate voice, "Eat your lunch, now!" followed by the familiar coos and giggles of an infant in response.

Lunch at ten at night?

This seemingly innocuous, random capture contributed greatly to our studies, prompting questions about the nature of time and differing realities between a spirit's existence and ours.

Speaking of which, when we ask outright for clues or straight answers to indicate what life is like from a spirit's perspective, we sometimes receive the very brusque, matter-of-fact response, "We're all dead," as if existing in that state is no big deal to them and there's nothing more to say about it.

This brings us to the practice of conducting EVP sessions in the first place. Depending on who is present (in spirit), most of the time those that reply really don't seem to know anything more of "the bigger picture" than what they are perceiving and experiencing themselves! This lends credence to Richard's Memory Matrix theory, in that it makes sense that a spirit person will only appreciate their own personal reality bubble and be completely content existing there, feeling no need to progress elsewhere, let alone make inquiries for themselves to share with us when we ask.

As with anything in life, nothing ventured is nothing gained. Incorporating EVP sessions into your investigation may feel like folly, but who is to say where or when you might meet those one or two spirit persons who will actually provide further insights? Don't lose hope. Persistence does pay.

A Note on EVPs (and Why Many Don't Make Sense)

Many times, it is clear that the message in an EVP is not for the investigator. We sometimes find this leads the investigator to automatically jump to the conclusion that the haunting is residual and not that of an intelligent spirit. Remember that spirits within a haunted building are not standing around waiting for you to show up. They are interacting with each other and doing things regardless of whether you are there or not. They don't simply exist for your convenience.

So, the next time you judge a spirit to be "residual" instead of "intelligent," consider the fact that perhaps whatever is present doesn't *want* to talk to you for their own reasons.

Spirit Boxes

The release of "Frank's Box" by paranormal enthusiast Frank Sumption (1953–2014) in 2002 gave rise to the mass production of the P-SB7 and P-SB11 devices that are readily available for purchase today. Every hard-nosed skeptic with a passing interest in debunking new developments in paranormal-based technology has been quick to label these instrumental transcommunication devices as the contemporary version of the spirit board and the output received as audio pareidolia and coincidence.

We invite skeptics to experience what we and many others have encountered in the field. As with scrutinizing photographs, auditory pareidolia is something an audio analyst should be aware of and wise enough to discount at all times.

While skeptics believe that coincidence also plays a role in the interpretations of spirit box output, they fail to explain how it is that clear, whole sentences spoken by the same voice are heard through these devices, when dozens of radio bandwidths are being scanned anywhere between 150 and 500 milliseconds a sweep. Two clear words should be an impossibility alone, yet when we invited a pair of podcasters to a site we'd investigated several times and conducted a spirit box session, one of its friendlier residents ("Anna") clearly inquired, "Who are these two?"

For those of us not blessed with strong psychic talents, other than portal gimmicks, the contemporary versions of the spirit box and P-SB7 and P-SB11 devices are, in our opinion, the closest technical means we have to establishing some form of real-time communication with spirits and other entities existing on a frequency outside our own.

By no means is this method of communication foolproof. There are mitigating factors that determine the effectiveness and success rate of a spirit box session, including the proximity of the device to particularly strong radio frequencies, overall speed of the bandwidth sweep, and the willingness or abilities of the spirit energies to reply coherently. It is, after all, a two-way street.

Keep in mind that anything that comes from a spirit box session never constitutes proof of ghost phenomena on its own. Since TSG has employed these devices in the field, we have recorded many sessions wherein replies have been coincidentally relevant and pertain to the questions asked or the history of the investigation site.

We have yet to meet another paranormal team that has realized that more than sporadic replies to investigators' questions come from a spirit box session and that there are at least four frequency levels to pay attention to when analyzing a session recording (see below).

In our experience of carefully and painstakingly analyzing recordings of our spirit box sessions, we have learned to discern and dismiss nonsensical output and have occasionally discovered conversations that seem to take place outside the replies or statements that were intentionally directed toward us. It's as if activating the spirit box is similar to having a genuinely talented medium or clairvoyant present. Spirits seem to recognize that the device is a viable means of being heard by the living and are drawn closer out of curiosity to use it for themselves.

For example, we may ask after a female spirit and receive a reply in a woman's voice. But then a male's voice will chime in and either tell us off or shout the woman's name in a stern-sounding tone as if warning her not to say any more. Behind the foreground spirit participants, we may hear laughter, cautionary comments, or snide criticisms shared between other spirits or even references to us.

Many of these conversations are typically discarded by most analysts because, on the surface, they are not cooperative, interactive replies to the investigators.

Like EVP responses, recorded spirit box sessions deserve to be scrutinized carefully. This is why we will never recommend the use of a "portal" device that claims to filter out the outside frequencies and focus potential replies toward the strongest, loudest channels. These devices, often sold for hundreds of dollars and encased inside antique radio cabinetry or speakers decorated with wire mesh and neon lights, do more to appease investigators who are impatient and want answers to come through quickly and definitively. They work best as tools for reality TV shows and live-streaming podcasts to incite extra jolts of excitement in the moment. The investigator is seriously missing out on a slew of information that is being blocked or warped further by the portal devices.

During our many years of analyzing spirit box audio, we have discovered at least four layers of radio frequencies within any given emission. Similar to the way we categorize EVP recordings (class A, B, and so on), these layers vary in quality, but they are present, and the untrained, impatient ear will easily miss them. The top two layers are the loudest, closest-sounding frequencies that can readily be heard by the naked ear, and these are the ones most investigators respond to during Q and A sessions. The third and fourth layers get progressively quieter and can be detected using quality headphones. Interestingly, words that are spoken on these levels are extremely faint and remarkably clearer than the obvious ones emitted from the louder upper tiers.

Conducting a Spirit Box Session

Just as with an EVP session, always use at least two digital recorders to log a spirit box session. Place one within a foot of the external speaker connected to the spirit box and a second approximately one to two feet away. The closer recorder will capture every nuance to come from the spirit box emission, while the secondary recorder will capture the most obvious output, much like the unaided human ear does. The recordings can be compared with each other later, which is especially useful when audio pareidolia needs to be considered or questioned. You may be amazed by how the recordings of the same session sometimes differ from one another. On rare occasions, we've received responses to questions that sound different between recordings and are sensible or logical replies relevant to the questions asked.

During the session, everyone present must remain silent and keep their bodies still for the benefit of the recording so noise contamination does not factor into the audio analysis. Establish who will ask the questions. If everyone takes a turn asking a question, allow at least ten seconds of team silence between them.

Once the team is settled, explain aloud to any spirits that may be listening what the spirit box device is intended to do and how they may be able to manipulate it to communicate with you. Activate the spirit box, find a band sweep (forward or backward) and speed that emits as much white noise static as possible, and begin your session.

If this is the first time a spirit box has been introduced to a field location, you may find it will take some time for the spirits to figure out what the device does and how they can use it. Be patient. Allow some time for the learning curve. We have found that once a spirit box has been utilized often in the same location, we will receive voices that greet us immediately upon activation of the device, before a single question is asked.

If your spirit box session will not be filmed and several people will be asking questions, it's a good idea that each person first identifies themselves aloud for the benefit of the digital recorder. This will help disseminate who said what during the analysis stage. As always, if someone on the team makes a noise shifting themselves or (in Peter's case) their stomach gurgles, be sure to tag the nonparanormal occurrence for the benefit of analysis later.

Unless you find yourselves establishing a genuine, lengthy dialogue, keep your spirit box sessions relatively brief. Truly careful analysis of each recording will take hours, so limit your sessions anywhere from ten to fifteen minutes for each recording. Besides, we have found the noise generated by spirit boxes seems to upset some ghosts, and we're not there to make enemies of those we wish to glean information from, are we?

Analyzing a Spirit Box Session
When analyzing a spirit box recording, use quality noise-canceling headphones and a computer or device that plays WAV or MP3 files back at a high output level for clarity's sake. Find a time of day inside a quiet room that will help concentrate your focus toward the task at hand.

Upon initial playback of the audio file, find a comfortable volume level during the spirit box output segment that doesn't make your ears bleed. Become accustomed to the range of audio you're hearing through the headphones before you experiment with increasing the volume to listen for the sounds that are running deeper.

In our experience, we have recorded EVPs in addition to the output coming from the spirit box, so be prepared for that possibility and ready to discern what was coming from the speaker of the spirit box and what was recorded apart from the radio signals at the time of the session.

As you will observe from the examples included here, our analyses and reports incorporate the time codes of the recording file. These make returning to key points easier and mark the time between investigator-made sounds and anomalous recordings, which is also interesting information to have handy. From this, one may detect recognizable patterns in fieldwork or results.

Sometimes, multiple voices will come through the spirit box that overlap each other, as if one or two other people are eager to blurt information *or* purposely cut across the voice of the primary responder to stop them from sharing more. We find all of these results fascinating, of course, and including details such as response times and voice intonations ultimately serve to enhance your final analyses. When someone reads your report, they'll have a much better understanding of the emotional human interactions (yours and spirits') that took place during the investigation.

Have more than one team member analyze these recordings separately. To avoid influencing your teammates' interpretation of what they're hearing, do not share your findings until each member has finished their analysis. This practice will go a long way to defend your results from skeptics' accusations of audio pareidolia.

Be honest with your interpretations when analyzing. Do your best to unravel statements that blurt out from the spirit box, but if they're not obvious and you find you have to work particularly hard at deciphering nonsensical noise, just say so. Ultimately, your critics will respect you more for your frankness.

Do not discount statements that do not seem to be part of the Q and A. Note every discernible word or exclamation, who says them (male, female, child), how they convey them (happily, bluntly, angrily) and when they happen (using the time code). Sometimes these words are part of a larger statement that is challenging to broadcast clearly from their side while the words of other speakers are broadcast more quickly in between. This phenomenon may speak to the layers or levels discussed earlier—spirits broadcasting from different levels may need to work harder at being noticed than others.

You may even hear ambient sounds as you analyze your spirit box sessions. We have recorded sessions where angry-sounding voices have told us to "Get out!" or "That's enough!" followed by the sound of a loud slap, a door slamming closed, or a heavy object being dropped (naturally interpreted as expressions of frustration or anger). On one occasion, after our client handed us a disused pistol that was discovered on their property, disembodied gunshots rang out from the spirit box during a particularly intense session.

Music (orchestral or that of a single instrument) will sometimes drift through a spirit box sweep. If this continues at regular intervals, it will be obvious it's coming from a station specializing in broadcasting music, so adjust the sweep rate to eliminate this accordingly. If music is infrequent or heard in possible response to an investigator question ("Which instrument can you play?"), this could be a shorthand reply a spirit person has borrowed from one of those aforementioned stations since it is easier to convey than trying to be heard vocally.

We realize that to the uninitiated, the idea of using a little imagination to explain some things that are recorded may not seem to be pure scientific validation and therefore is easy fodder for the closed-minded skeptics, but admitting to your most educated guesses (rather than claiming them as facts) is a part of what makes us human and will go a long way to help answer the overall mystery we're trying so hard to solve. (Arguably, without imagination, how many other accepted scientific advances would humankind be missing out on?)

In short, be sure to include these and other environmental noises in your analysis report, too.

A Note on Spirit Box Responses (and Why Many Don't Make Sense)
When analyzing spirit box session recordings, be prepared for results that differ from common dialogue exchanges between physical human beings.

Not only do spirit box devices tend to eavesdrop on otherworldly conversations that have nothing to do with you, your team, or your investigation goals, but when a spirit box is introduced to a haunted location, its presence might inspire latent spirits to speak up—sometimes all at once.

Just as mediums are unexpectedly inundated with eager spirit participants, the spirit box seems to attract the same kind of attention. As a result, your unfiltered spirit box recordings should resemble a cacophony of statements and interjections spouted within split seconds of each other but not necessarily connected in a sensible pattern. (Note that "unfiltered," in this case, means not emitted through software or portal devices designed to clarify what they deem as relevant data.)

Here is a sampling of a real-life spirit box session conducted within a particularly active location. In the span of a few seconds, there proved to be a mix of direct responses to us and a heated conflict between "them":

Richard: Hello?

Spirit box (unknown gender): Hello.

Richard: How are you?

Spirit box (female, pleasant): Fine.

Spirit box (male, gruff): Go to hell!

Richard: My name's Richard. What's your name?

Spirit box (male, immediate): Chris!

Spirit box: We heard them.

Spirit box (young male, Scottish accent): That's enough!

Spirit box (young female, exclaiming): Jesus!

Spirit box (unknown gender): Alena!

Peter: What is your name?

Spirit box (young female, immediate): David!

Spirit box (male, gruff): Alena!

Spirit box: [Loud burst of static resembling china breaking]

Spirit box: [Woman's shriek]

Spirit box (unknown gender, shouting): Go!

Though our skeptics will immediately accuse us of incorporating audio pareidolia into our findings, you'll note that the direct answers to our questions did in fact materialize, albeit in between a barrage of other noise.

Again, don't discount the noise surrounding the desirable replies. These may be comments directed toward the spirits who are willing to participate and in effect may introduce new ghost presences into the investigative mix as well.

This is why we staunchly discourage using a portal device that purports to weed out "garbage" noise; doing so is detrimental to a serious investigation. By using a portal version of a spirit box, you're essentially trusting that the built-in filter will faithfully distinguish the differences between wanted and unwanted information to further your cause.

The exact same principle applies to investigation teams employing the Estes Method, in which an investigator is blindfolded and focuses their complete attention on listening to spirit box output through noise-canceling headphones, relaying phrases or words they think they are hearing at random. (See "The Spirit Box Ganzfeld Experiment" in chapter 1.)

We are confident you'll find that just a little extra time and legwork performing careful analysis of recorded spirit box sessions will reap far richer rewards, data-wise.

Anomalous Presence-Detecting Using Technology

EMF meters are a valuable part of the investigator's gear. These include proximity meters that alert the team to electromagnetic energy "pockets" via light and sound alarms.

These kinds of meters include the REM pod, the Mel meter, E. probes, EDI meters, flux responsive devices, the BooBuddy (a teddy bear with built-in EMF detectors), the 360 Parascope, and, more recently, the Trip-Wire (available in twelve- or thirty-six-foot lengths) and para-light mini lanterns. None of these devices are examples of new technology. Rather, they are imaginative designs utilizing basic electromagnetic detection mechanics.

As when using gauss meters, a serious paranormal investigator cannot say with any degree of scientific certainty they are detecting the presence of a ghost when using such devices. The alerts are being triggered by a sudden change in the surrounding environment.

However, an exception can be made when a proximity meter is activated in direct response to questions posed by the investigator. Each team's queries will vary, but a typical introductory line of questioning may include:

+ If there's someone with us right now, would you please touch or stand near that device?
+ Are you able to activate some or all the lights when you get close to it?
+ Please make the device light up green if your answer is yes, red for no. Are you able to do that?
+ Do you mind if we converse with you?
+ Are you a man/woman/boy/girl?
+ Do you mind sharing your age? I'm _____ years old. Are you twenty or older?

✦ We come as guests in your space and would like to know with whom we're speaking.

✦ Since we find it difficult to hear you clearly, if I recite the alphabet, are you comfortable using this device to spell your name out?

Be sure to ask respectful questions that supply you with data that can be verified as soon as possible. Try not to dwell on small talk, as your spirit host may tire of performing for you and opt to halt communication.

Only when an unseen force exhibiting a degree of intelligence or understanding is responding in the moment can we speculate that the ghost of a person is likely present.

Additional Environment-Sensitive Gear

Electromagnetic energy isn't the only measurable element a spirit can affect.

A search of the ghost-hunting marketplace will reveal other devices that indicate or are activated by sudden temperature differences (FLIR thermal cameras), ultrasound noise (paranormal music boxes), and even vibrations and air pressure changes (EDI+ meters). These can be utilized in Q and A sessions using a little imagination, creativity, and patience.

Additionally, ion detectors and Geiger counters are handy to have when measuring environmental differences throughout an investigation, though they are extremely expensive.

Obsolete and Questionable Gear

The following are electronic devices that were once available to aspiring investigators but have either been discontinued, are in the process of becoming dated (as of this writing), or are simply questionable in terms of offering legitimate field evidence.

The **Ovilus** (pronounced AH-VEH-LUS) is manufactured and distributed by American engineer Bill Chappell's Digital Dowsing. This series of instrumentation purports to interpret environmental changes (thermal heat and IR, UV, and visible light) and convert them into words or phrases, suggesting that spirit people utilize them in order to converse with investigators in real time. With preset databases of thousands of words (in English and Spanish), the Ovilus would appear to be *the* must-have device for every serious team that can afford one (seriously, the Ovilus 3+ retails at fifteen hundred dollars). Our own experiments with the original Ovilus 3 in the field have proven fruitless at best. Though Digital Dowsing claims none of their Ovilus or talking devices use random word generators, the nonsensical output *we've* encountered has inspired our team to dub this gadget the "Paranormal Speak 'n' Spell." The bottom line: Be careful that wishful thinking on your part doesn't supersede common sense when seemingly relevant answers come from an Ovilus. The odds of simple coincidence are greater than actual evidence.

Variations utilizing similar technology include the Paranormal Puck, BooBuddy Ghost Hunting Bear, and the Onvoy Ghost Box Communicator.

The **RT-EVP** digital recorder was developed and retailed in 2010 by Mel meter, REM pod, and P-SB7 inventor Gary Galka. The RT-EVP recorder (*RT* standing for "real time") was the first (and only) digital recorder marketed toward investigators, capable of detecting sound frequencies at 15 Hz and boosting them into the human hearing range of 20 Hz. This device (and a later version, the RT-EVP-XTR) included left and right audio alert indicators, a white noise generator, and the ability for a user to connect headphones to it and listen for disembodied voices while recording simultaneously.

Sadly, we must refer to this outstanding piece of technology in the past tense, as its manufacture was discontinued in 2014. Hardware issues and multiple user complaints regarding awkward access to the device's various features through its menu likely played a huge role in the RT-EVP's demise. Until the technological kinks are resolved and a markedly improved reissue is available, we will handle *our* team RT-EVP recorder with kid gloves and pray that it never malfunctions.

In the not-too-distant past, someone hit upon the idea to utilize the **Kinect structured-light sensor (SLS)** device from their Xbox gaming system and apply it to the ghost-seeking field. The sight of human-shaped bodies depicted as animated stick figures appearing in otherwise empty spaces (sometimes moving in response to investigator requests) stirred the imagination and introduced an exciting, albeit cumbersome, piece of field tech.

The Searcher Group has had the opportunity to work with this device with mixed outcomes. Some detections seemed like promising hits, while others were obvious misinterpretations by the system software in its bid to try to make sense of its environs. We're of the mindset that if your team owns one, it is still worthwhile to experiment with the Kinect SLS camera system. We recommend locking it in a stationary position, as opposed to walking about with it, to maximize the potential for credible hits. Treat any potential hits as cautionary evidence to be corroborated with EVPs, medium testimony, factual site history, and so on before you declare the figure(s) you've captured are absolute proof of anything truly ghostly.

Probably the simplest, most accessible, and most affordable means to experiment with spirit communication using electronic tech involves miniature incandescent or **LED flashlights**. The idea is to activate each flashlight, then loosen the connections between bulbs and battery terminals to the point that the light goes out but will illuminate when it experiences the slightest pressure.

Using this as a makeshift proximity meter hack, and a means of proving that an intelligent energy form is responding to your questions by activating and deactivating the lights, may appear to work successfully both on TV and in actual practice, but there's a physical reason for those responses, and it ain't paranormal.

In fact, the explanation is so complex, we recommend you visit YouTube user verklagekasper and watch his tutorial called "Ghost Hunting Flashlight Trick: Physical Explanation and Experiments," posted in 2012.

We admit that before we were aware of its public debunking, we, too, experimented with the flashlight technique, always running it concurrently with surveillance or digital recorders in a bid to capture corroborating audio-visual evidence. Now that we are all the more wiser, we suggest no one waste precious field time or battery energy continuing to pursue this particular practice.

The theory that ghosts are comprised of electromagnetic energy, and therefore seek sources of electromagnetic energy in order to both exist and to manifest themselves, has largely continued to persist since the early 2000s and the advent of ghost-hunting reality TV. While we wholeheartedly advocate for new ideas to consider, discuss, and test in the field, unfortunately this particular notion has yet to be proven over twenty years later.

One device, marketed as an **EM pump**, is designed to attract invisible entities, effectively feed them, and thereby provoke manifestations by emitting strong waves of electromagnetic energy. A theoretical side benefit is that by incorporating EM pumps, spirits will be dissuaded from draining the batteries powering the investigators' electronic gear. The Searcher Group has experimented with using EM pumps extensively, and apart from one location where the device itself was toyed with by someone unseen, we cannot conclude with certainty that this apparatus works as it should. We will continue to have our supply of pumps on hand, but until we see unquestionable results, we'll categorize the EM pump as questionable technology.

Low-Budget Technology

As volunteers, members of TSG have gradually added to their field gear kits when personal finances allow. However, anomaly detection is historically rooted in a number of simpler and significantly more affordable methods. Do not be afraid to employ any of these techniques, especially in tandem with your electrical and battery-operated equipment.

First employed by pioneering investigator Harry Price (1881–1948), the practice of **spreading talcum powder**, baby powder, or flour over an area of suspected paranormal traffic has proven to be a very effective, albeit messy, means of capturing physical proof of unseen forces at work. Over several years of utilizing this approach, TSG has secured imprints of a fashionable boot including its manufacturer's logo, a slipper including the owner's overhanging toe prints, and letters of the alphabet scrawled through the layer of powder by disembodied persons.

In a dry, controlled indoor location without a source of wind, tape black garbage bags down on the floor as flat as possible over a specific area and spread a generous, even layer of white powder across the surface. Use a small paintbrush to even the powder out as best as possible. Once deployed, take control photos and/or monitor the area using a surveillance camera. Ideally, the team should avoid traveling through this area throughout the investigation. If a surveillance camera is unavailable to monitor the powder, appoint a member to check and document the area with photo updates every half hour to help determine an approximate time frame should something interact with the powder.

Deploying this powder trap in a damp environment (e.g., a concrete or stone basement floor or a restroom) for a lengthy period of time will likely result in the powder clumping together, with cracks forming in the surface as the material absorbs moisture from its surroundings.

Be forewarned that successful results are not guaranteed and that you must deploy this powder "trap" fully prepared to dispose of the residual mess after a thorough sweeping or by using a portable vacuum cleaner. It's a good idea to ask your client if they're comfortable with you experimenting with this technique first. Assure them your team will clean up after itself.

A variation on the use of powder is using sugar instead, as suggested and used by veteran paranormal investigator and parapsychologist Peter Underwood (1923–2014). The adhesive property of sugar crystals causes the material to stick to anything that comes in contact with it and in theory be pulled away from the area (and perhaps deposited outside it) by a traveling entity—or detected on the shoes of someone perpetuating a hoax.

Since 3000 BC, humankind has lived with some form of wind chime. Whether they are used to ward off birds or evil spirits or to create a symphony of pleasurable sound, **wind chimes** should immediately be recognizable to most spirit people residing on the site you are investigating. As such, wind chimes are natural trigger objects, as well as easily manipulated alarm systems for our purposes. Introducing a set of wind chimes, especially to a troubled location that was likely devoid of this calming, healing instrument, may inspire curiosity or trigger memories of happier times on the ghosts' part, motivating interaction with them. Spirit children are very likely to be tempted to do so if encouraged.

Choose some chimes that are long enough to pack and transport handily, light enough that they can be moved without too much effort, and yet not so light that any slight breeze, such as that from a person walking past them, will set them swinging. Peter uses a set of glass chimes and finds himself constantly teased by the team when he hangs them from an old floor-model lampstand he purchased from a thrift store.

As with the powder trap, results are not always forthcoming and much depends on the intensity of spirit activity. Still, in one instance, the chimes were heard clinking loudly from the ground floor while the entire team was investigating the second floor of a Victorian-era farmhouse. In another case, several witnesses watched in amazement as the middle three chimes swung freely while the outer chimes remained still, in conjunction with a spirit box session in the basement of a former town hall.

Suspending a series of **small bells** along a string and placing them away from investigator traffic makes for a smaller, easier-to-carry version of a wind chime and can be utilized as both a trip wire across thresholds ghosts are reported to travel and a trigger object.

Perhaps the simplest, most economical, easiest-to-carry electromagnetic field–detecting device is a **pendulum**. As a variation on the sixteenth-century dowsing technique, it takes a steady hand to ensure a pendulum's swing is not influenced by its user and the ideomotor effect (unconscious muscle spasms in reaction to a person's expectations or ideas). The best way to ensure an investigator is not influencing its movement is to hang the pendulum to dangle freely underneath a tripod. Pendulums can be used on their own or in tandem with a set of letters and numbers laid out underneath them like a spirit board.

A **spirit board** is a divination device dating back to ancient Greece. It is more popularly known by its brand name: Ouija (pronounced WEE-JAH). Letters of the alphabet, numerals from zero to nine, short answers (yes/no), and salutations (hello/goodbye) are printed or placed on a flat surface. A planchette (French for "little plank" or "table") placed over the written icons is seemingly influenced by spirit presences and moves to answer the users' questions and spell messages accordingly.

Science and skeptics credit the ideomotor effect to explain the planchette's movement, while hard-nosed believers attribute replies to spirit attempts to communicate. The Searcher Group is open to both explanations but is also aware of the possibility of imbuing the spirit board device with the power of human intent, much like physical religious objects or lucky charm icons.

It's a good idea to ask your client if they're comfortable with you experimenting with this device first. Popular media (and perhaps personal experience) has effectively demonized the use and mere presence of spirit boards, so utilizing one may make your clients uneasy. Carefully explain your reasons and philosophy for introducing a spirit board to your investigation beforehand.

When an EMF reader isn't handy, have a **magnetic compass** ready to scan for anomalous needle readings. One evening, while working on a particularly challenging case, the team Richard was working with felt a discernible foreboding in the backyard of a residence bordering a forest. Placing his handheld compass on the ground, Richard observed the needle refuse to settle on magnetic north over a period of ten minutes. Once the overwhelming presence was no longer sensed, the needle slowed and the compass functioned properly.

Fans of board games created and sold in North America will appreciate the **Pop-O-Matic die roller**, a six-sided die encased within a transparent plastic bubble that rests on a floor of flexible metal. When the dome is depressed and then released, the metal floor snaps and sends the die ricocheting within the confines of the bubble until it settles, displaying a new number. Variations of this gizmo have appeared since its initial introduction as part of the Kohner Bros. board game *Trouble* (1965) and makes for an instantly recognizable and relatable trigger object.

Inspired by past laboratory tests of telekinesis, wherein a subject was tasked to move an enclosed object using their mind, Peter introduced a Pop-O-Matic bubble to a particularly active investigation site, demonstrated how it worked, and left it overnight, monitored by a digital recorder. Returning to retrieve his gear hours later, Peter was disappointed to note the die inside the bubble had not moved an iota. However, later analysis of the audio recording revealed something or someone had mimicked the familiar pop-rattle-settling sound of the bubble being activated. This sound had been captured more than once. (Had Peter recorded someone's memory of the Pop-O-Matic sound?)

Perhaps it was familiarity that excited the spirit of a silently observing female or child when teammate James McCulloch demonstrated how to use the Pop-O-Matic in the course of a different investigation. On this occasion, James called aloud the top-facing number to inspire a ghostly copycat reaction we could catch on our recorders. The ploy worked; James called, "One!" before depressing the bubble. As the die settled, an excited, youthful-sounding voice captured as a clear EVP exclaimed, "Two!" as if gleefully anticipating the next logical number. As it turned out, the ghost's shout was premature—the die landed on four.

Utilizing the age-old superstition or theory that mirrors have the ability to trap and effectively hold a person's spirit indefinitely (See "Mirrors" in chapter 1), the **Devil's Toy Box**, a low-budget device, was conceived in the late 2000s and is easy to construct yourself.

Simply seal six square-shaped mirrors together to form a cube, mirror sides turned inward to face each other, and you have yourself a handheld psychomanteum to invite spirits to enter and theoretically imprison themselves. A variation of this device, introduced by Digital Dowsing in 2006, featured a small microphone secured inside the box in the hope that EVPs might be recorded by ghosts that entered. While a logical idea, surprisingly Digital Dowsing's version was devoid of a complete seal of its edges, even including a gap to allow for wiggle room of the microphone wire protruding from the interior, and could be opened from one side. This lack of a true mirrored 360-degree enclosure would (theoretically) ensure that any spirit energy had more than enough room to escape before any results might be logged.

If your team decides to utilize a properly sealed mirror box device, consider investing in a pick-up microphone and using the suction cup to seal the mic to the exterior of the box to record any sounds that might emanate from inside it. Be sure to log baseline EMF and static readings of the box before, during, and after it is used in the field, noting the differences—if any. The Searcher Group once situated a mirror box on the site of an alleged portal and placed a digital recorder on top. While we failed to seize an ectoplasmic entity traveling on its way through the purported opening, the recorder captured the sound of someone kicking at the box, missing it, and striking a hard surface nearby.

If your team chooses to incorporate this device, we strongly suggest that no one refers to it as the Devil's Toy Box, especially in front of an anxious client. Explain the principal theory behind its simple design but call it a mirror box, phantom box, or anything less fear-inducing than an association with universally recognized evil.

Anyone who has had the pleasure of opening a carton packed with **Styrofoam peanuts** or chips will appreciate the thinking behind their use in the investigation field. It was the sight of a coworker pulling his Styrofoam-covered arm from inside a crate full of these static-charged polystyrene chips that influenced Richard to experiment with them during the team's Fusion Mansion investigation in 2008.

To prevent drafts from affecting the outcome, Richard closed and sealed off every door before emptying an industrial bag of Styrofoam peanuts along the length of one side of the second-floor hall. Leaving a surveillance camera to monitor the chips from the other end of the hallway, the team retreated to work elsewhere on the property.

Returning a couple hours later, the team was excited to find dozens of Styrofoam chips now clinging along the height of a locked door at the end of the hall. They were dismayed, however, to find someone had deactivated the camera before the peanuts would have been filmed theoretically clinging to an invisible person walking through them on their way to passing through that locked door.

While the Styrofoam static test showed definite promise in this case, the tedium and frustration of cleaning up after this particular experiment may dissuade other teams from trying it for themselves.

The Trigger Effect

Most people with an interest in ghost investigation are familiar with the term *trigger object*, which refers to ordinary portable items that are purposely introduced to an allegedly haunted site with the intent to evoke a recorded response by an unseen entity. This tactical experiment definitely works, as professional and thrill-seeking teams worldwide will readily attest, and it provides results that most closed-minded skeptics rarely have an explanation for (outside questioning the integrity of the object's initial placement).

The items you choose should vary by location and their respective histories. Some objects are universally recognizable and can be acquired from your own home or a modern-day source, but to help gain the trust of a wary spirit, you can easily communicate your appreciation for the era they originated from by using items and brands that were likely most familiar to them and their everyday experiences.

Employing trigger objects that serve dual purposes helps to relieve some of the bulk of the investigator's tool kit, such as the aforementioned wind chimes, Pop-O-Matic die bubble, and BooBuddy teddy bear toy. These items are not only attractive and intriguing to approach but will indicate unseen presences via sound and lights.

Some commonly used objects include dolls, balls, marbles, wooden vehicles, dice, playing cards, coins, chocolate, alcohol, paper and pencil (or a charcoal stick), and bells.

Include graph paper in your kit to place underneath small trigger objects and trace an outline of the item onto the paper before leaving them alone. Like using the powder trap, if you don't have a spare camera to monitor the trigger object, document the article's placement photographically and have a team member check on it and photograph it every half hour or so.

In places where keyboard instruments have been reported to play on their own, we have brought period-appropriate sheet music and placed it on the instrument's music rack to appeal to resident pianists or organists.

Incorporating era-appropriate music at some point during your investigation is a must-try in terms of trigger experimentation. At its most basic, music is a universally appreciated set of frequencies that affects our deepest senses, including our emotions, and triggers memory recall connected to those emotions. Varying degrees of reactions are bound to manifest when coaxing memories from spirits via familiar music. We've experienced a tangible mood change throughout an entire building, the sobs of a woman picked up as

EVP in a restored 1800s era farmhouse parlor, and the disembodied voice of a young girl belting out the lyrics to Franz Schubert's "Ave Maria" (1825).

If you are enough fortunate to investigate sites with a particularly long history of human traffic (theatres, dance halls, hotels) and you're not sure which era to focus on, try several genres of music over the course of many investigations to determine which choices elicit responses. Peter compiled a CD of vintage hit parade melodies to play partway through a town hall investigation and was rewarded with several EVP responses, including a male saying "dancing" while an upbeat tune played and another male commenting sarcastically, "Peter, you can do better than that" when Bing Crosby's voice crooned "White Christmas."

In theory, introducing the popular toy Etch A Sketch to an investigation site makes sense. As a trigger object, the hope, of course, is that a spirit person will recognize this device, which has been around since the 1960s, and be inspired to scrawl a message in the screen through the fine layer of aluminum powder that coats it. Contrary to beliefs that aluminum is inherently magnetic (it's not), one may consider utilizing this toy in the field. If ghosts can manipulate flour and talc, why not aluminum powder?

For all of the experiments we share here, expect that nothing will happen, so that when something *does*, your drive to keep experimenting will be inspired tenfold. Also remember that just because a certain experiment appears to fail in one location, this doesn't mean it won't elicit a promising result at another.

Chapter 4
PRE-INVESTIGATION

Now we've reached what most people entering this field of study look forward to the most: The investigation itself. However, while the idea of visiting someone else's property after hours to run experiments and hope for evidence-worthy "hits" feels exciting and rife with unknown possibilities, there first remains protocol and procedure to consider in preparation for this crucial stage.

Types of Investigations

Most people in this field call themselves paranormal investigators, which is only slightly accurate regarding what they do. When one "investigates," they are exploring, examining, inspecting, probing, and generally "nosing around" to discover truth behind a crime or a problem.

As a paranormal investigator with a focus on soul survival and life after death, ghosts, and hauntings, there are two types of investigations:

The call for help investigation is self-explanatory; the team responds to a request for assistance made by a person (or group of people) who reports an issue related to what they perceive as paranormal in nature. This may include any number of locations, such as a home or a place of business. The intent of most people reaching out is for an investigator to validate what has been experienced by the complainant. In some cases, a resolution may be requested.

Pure research, however, is the intentional investigation of a property either known to be or rumored to be haunted, with the express purpose to gain insights into paranormal activity, develop and test various theory through experimentation, and make valid discovery and collect any available evidence of phenomena.

The calls for help are often the more challenging cases, simply because the investigator must work directly with the people involved, making it extremely difficult to control the environment. Timelines between clients and investigators are usually rushed, and privacy issues require constant consideration.

The pure research investigation is easier to control. Timelines are relaxed, and site access is usually open and flexible. Rarely does the investigator need to be concerned about outsider involvement.

Committing to Investigations

To provide the best possible investigation into an alleged haunting the team must (1) use best practices and (2) control the data and location as best as possible.

All too often a client's call for help with an alleged haunted location includes an expectation that the investigating team will conclusively resolve their perceived issue. This is commonly done without the client making a commitment to assist in the resolution of their situation.

The best way to proceed with an active investigation is to explore all possibilities, and this can only be done with commitment from the client to achieve this goal. To establish the existence of any paranormal activity, all other normal, explainable possibilities must be eliminated.

Understand that hallucinations can present themselves under many different circumstances, and any such occurrences must be investigated as vigorously and thoroughly as any other suspected paranormal event would be.

Just as the investigative team commits to making all possible attempts to validate and possibly resolve a haunting, so must the client commit to eliminating medical reasons for experienced events. This can be accomplished with a thorough examination by their family doctor.

The investigator will—if well equipped and possessing the proper skills—investigate the location for toxic mold, high levels of electromagnetic fields, carbon monoxide, and infrasound. If the skills or equipment are not available, a professional home inspector should be consulted.

Once all these areas are explored and no natural cause is found for the occurrences, a full investigation should follow using strict protocols.

Finding Locations and Gaining Access

Obviously, none of us can do our jobs as researchers if we don't have access to data. If invitations from homeowners or business owners to investigate their properties are not immediately forthcoming, you must take the initiative and connect with those who own or manage places of particular interest yourself.

There is another option, which immediately sets the thrill-seekers apart from the professionals, and we will *never* welcome this alternative in our dojo: Trespassing to conduct an investigation. Never resort to this.

Apart from the serious legal repercussions if caught trespassing, team safety—and that of the site itself—is also at stake. Most areas cordoned off to discourage foot traffic are done so for a reason; there are likely hidden physical dangers that may harm or even kill an uninvited wanderer looking for a late-night thrill to brag about later. Even if the extent of team injuries is minimal, how will those group members react when nothing of a paranormal nature occurs? Many will act out of impatience, malice, or impaired judgment (i.e., influenced by drugs or alcohol) and proceed to destroy some or all aspects of the property before leaving it.

It is equally important to realize that every time a trespasser claims to be a "ghost hunter," they inflict irreparable damage on the field of legitimate research—at least a thousandfold (conservatively speaking). The decision to associate paranormal investigation with a legal infraction may make sensational media copy, but doing so effectively lumps them (and their reprehensible actions) with us in the court of public opinion.

As professionals, we must work extra hard not only to maintain our team standards on a consistent basis but also to educate the public, distance ourselves from the clowns with nothing to lose, and do our damnedest as a law-abiding team to reassure potential clients we have their very best interests at heart when we ask them to allow us on site.

If you are team leader, you must designate one member of the team as location manager. This person is responsible for clearly conveying the team's intent and protocols to potential clients, many of whom are not familiar with what a professional paranormal investigation entails. Ensure that you and the location manager agree on the respectful approach you wish to express to your potential clients in terms of the team's reliability and trustworthiness. Additionally, as team leader, insist on reviewing every email or phone message before it is delivered by the location manager to the potential client.

Over time, and after many such emails or phone calls, a point will be reached wherein the location manager will have proved themselves capable of representing the team accurately (and hopefully effectively) and that the team leader may wish to limit their own input, simply approving the intended client rather than proofreading the proposals of the location manager.

How to Start

Begin by familiarizing yourself with the location you believe might be a suitable candidate for a paranormal investigation. Ask yourself why this location may be home to spirits: Is it historic? Have people perished there (or nearby)? Is it a popular, beloved, or famous place that has seen and continues to see much foot traffic? Have you heard stories of people reporting ghost experiences associated with this place?

While you're exploring the practicality of conducting research on the site, try to gauge the space that is available for the team to cover, whether it is amenable to powering electrical equipment, its proximity to potential noise contamination, and whether the neighborhood is safe or policed, and so on. (Once you're actually on site, you may be shown areas you didn't know existed, let alone are accessible, but let's concentrate on getting you in first.)

Many publicly accessible places have websites. Scour these—along with flyers, pamphlets, and print advertisements—for any information about the site's history (whether ghosts are openly associated with it or not) and the mission statements they share (usually under a subheading titled "About Us"). People tend to feel happy when they perceive they've been heard. Your potential clients are naturally proud and extremely protective of their sites and are likely to appreciate hearing their words echoed back to them in the context of a formal introduction.

Try to assess the odds that the owners or managers of the site might be open to hearing from a reputable paranormal team like yours. Some historic sites may have been approached in the past (or have been stigmatized by our "friends," the trespassing vandals) and may already incorporate policies online discouraging other groups from doing so. If you come across this or a similar statement rejecting site access for this purpose, respect their wishes and move on to researching other possible locations.

In our experience, we have found locations that openly invite paranormal teams to explore their reputedly haunted properties—for a hefty admission fee. Every team is different, and your members might be willing to shell out hundreds of dollars for a limited, guarantee-less experience, but in The Searcher Group's case, we politely bow out and continue looking for an alternate site. As volunteers already sinking our pocket money into gear, batteries, travel, and food, we literally cannot afford to invest any further in endeavors like these.

Now, before composing and sending a request to investigate, there are a few things to keep in mind:

Know that unless the property owner has received multiple similar requests in the past, your message will stand out as an anomaly in that person's normal workday routine. This may actually work in your favor, as the person receiving your request will probably be surprised/amused/delighted at receiving it and may take extra care to respond in kind rather than let it sit in their inbox unattended.

Alternately, the recipient may not appreciate receiving it. At all. We once heard back from a property owner who wrote, "Unequivocally, absolutely NO, thank you." While the response was disappointing, this gentleman earned our respect for taking the time to reply, especially in such a succinct and passionate-sounding way! (More on this matter coming up.) Many letters of inquiry are never acknowledged.

In addition to the stigma and fear brought on by entertainment media, be prepared to accept that the property owner/manager may practice a religion that is at odds with our line of work, or they may have personal biases that will be triggered by your inquiry.

We are HUGE proponents of the adage "it never hurts to ask." So, with the aforementioned possible responses in mind, let's start composing your request.

What to Say

Now that you've done a bit of homework to assess the suitability of a location, it's time to draft your appeal to those in charge. The examples we'll share will be in the context of email correspondence. You may wish to adopt the following suggestions into a phone call or in-person conversation instead.

Keeping in mind that the people receiving your proposals are busy and preoccupied with their own lives and personal matters, you need to craft your statements succinctly and get to the point of the request as soon as possible—in a respectful manner, of course.

Consider also the fact that not everybody is familiar with the kind of work we do, in the least. To help paint the picture for them, try to summarize the investigation and post-investigation procedures clearly and in as unexciting a tone as possible.

If you have been referred to the client by a mutual acquaintance or member of their staff, be sure to include that person's name immediately. Doing so will engage their attention and help develop the client's trust in you, and therefore your accountability, by proxy.

Find a balance to pitch your case: Project confidence that your team is right for the job without coming across as arrogant or cocky.

Put forth your request to access the client's site and let them know you will be understanding and respectful—not only of the site but of their wishes and in handling the intelligence gathered after analyzing the investigation data. Treat every aspect of your request with sensitivity.

Assure the potential client that you are reliable and reputable. Provide references. You only have one shot at making a positive first impression. Aim to create the most appealing presentation you can.

Our standard TSG request letters have evolved over the years, and unfortunately, while we prefer not to boast, we have been forced to go one step further, citing proof of our accomplishments and credibility in order to distinguish ourselves from dubious ghost-hunting teams. If your team has earned some favorable press from respected media sources, you may want to provide hyperlinks to these articles to help your prospects.

Review and proofread the letter of intent before sending. (If you feel you are not adept at writing a detailed email or would prefer to use a different medium, arrange for a telephone call or live meeting to discuss your team's qualifications as professional investigators.)

Sending the Request

Your letter has been composed, it's been approved by the team leader, and you've chosen an appropriate time of day to reach your potential client. Time to hit *send*.

Now comes the fun part: The wait for a response, which will hopefully be a positive one. In our experience, if you don't receive an automatically generated reply acknowledging your email, it is rare to receive a reply of *any* kind the same day the proposal letter is sent. The client may be away on vacation, have personal matters to attend to, or be buried too deeply in work to dedicate the time it will take to completely absorb the content of your letter, so allow them some breathing space to attend to your request.

Sadly, in this day and age, many people won't do you the courtesy of acknowledging your attempt to reach them at all. Be prepared for that possibility and exercise patience.

Follow-Up Emails
We have learned to wait at least five to seven business days before sending a follow-up email, if we haven't received a response within that time.

Being Ignored or Rejected

You may find that—despite your team's respectability and qualifications—some replies will read quite aggressively. We have received rejections that have run the gamut from "A firm 'No,' thank you" to those of shortsighted CEOs who cannot fathom how they could potentially profit from collaborating with a credible volunteer group that would bring them free information (even though you've explained how).

In every case, even if you feel you have been ignored or led on over a long period of waiting, grit your teeth, count to thirteen, and take the proverbial high road, leading by example by responding quickly and pleasantly.

If you never hear back, you have a decision to make. Is this site worth risking pestering the owner(s) for? If not, then cut your losses and move on to a new prospect, repeating the procedure.

If these direct communication efforts continue to be rebuffed or you receive a resounding no to your request, walk away with your head held high, satisfied you've done everything possible to access that site.

Dealing with Heritage Organizations and Historical Societies

An obvious source of potential investigation work opportunities are trustees that oversee the maintenance and upkeep of historical homes and designated heritage properties.

In our bid to conduct our life-after-life studies within controlled settings, we have contacted several organizations dedicated to preserving cultural and architectural heritage. For our part, we explain that The Searcher Group has done its utmost to establish its credibility as a reliable, accomplished team of investigators; we guarantee safety and confidentiality and share our field findings with our clients, free of charge. What the client chooses to do with this information is up to them.

By reaching the committee heads, the hope, of course, is that they will endorse our team and convey word of our pro bono services to the membership of the organization. The further hope is that curious, open-minded owners of historical sites will be inspired to contact our team with offers of access.

The paranormal-minded among them will immediately appreciate the win-win scenario being offered; in exchange for them allowing you access, your team conducts a discreet and thorough investigation, free of charge. The results of the study are then shared with them, and they may in turn decide to capitalize on this information to increase visitor traffic. On the face of it, accepting this offer would appear to be an effort-free, low-risk, high-gain no-brainer on the part of heritage property owners. The historical site might sell a published account of your findings or use your investigation results to tap into people's interest in the paranormal by implementing ghost walks, hosting special after-hours events, or offering self-touring mobile apps.

However, because people serving on such committees and boards differ in terms of personal beliefs, backgrounds, and biases, our earnest, respectful inquiries aren't always understood, nor are our services appreciated, despite our best efforts to tactfully explain our intentions and alleviate fears of the unknown. For example, a respected local historian who personally shuns anything to do with the paranormal may negatively influence committee members' decisions to move forward in terms of associating with your team. The sensationalism of paranormal TV programs and news reports of vandals and trespassers purporting to be ghost hunters certainly do not help the earnest professional's proposal to be taken seriously. It is human nature to paint us with the same brush, after all.

In our experience, if we're not rejected outright, most responses are of the "Thank you for contacting us; we're not interested" kind, presumably sent by designated representatives who likely didn't confer with the organization's members to allow *them* to decide for themselves. In other cases, some heritage organizations adopt and implement a firm "No paranormal groups allowed" bylaw despite years of persistent, unexplainable experiences reported by their visitors.

Oddly, we have also observed these same organizations continuously plead for ideas to promote heritage awareness and sources of tourism income. Once, during a phone conversation with a province-wide heritage spokesperson, the individual rejected our offer to discuss how we could help, then flatly admitted that the organization she represented wasn't interested in what the public wanted, just funding from large corporations.

Regardless of individual organization heads' reasons for not taking advantage of your team's services, realize that for every hundred rejections, one or two attempts can prove successful, so continue to be persistent. Even when rejected, end communications on a polite and diplomatic note. Remember that as in any alliance, the members that comprise heritage organizations come and go; the mindset and attitude toward our work and the good that can come from it may change in your favor in the near future.

Next Steps

You receive a reply, and it's a yes from your new client. What next?

For one, you must NOT visit a social media platform and reveal the location where you will be investigating—not even the town or city, no matter how large the community may be. Unless the client has given you permission (which at this stage is highly unlikely), do not even offer tantalizing clues as to where you will be exploring. That knowledge is confidential and reserved for families and partners at home hoping they won't receive a call from police or a hospital while you're away investigating.

Since the proverbial ball is in the client's figurative court, respond to the client with gratitude and arrange a time to meet to discuss particulars ahead of the investigation, if possible. Invite the client to join the investigation if they wish to, and politely discourage them from inviting any other non-investigators. After all, this is not exactly a more-the-merrier kind of visit you'll be undertaking, and you are not there to entertain. Inform them that you recommend keeping the number of people present limited for accurate data-collection purposes.

If the site is a great distance away and you cannot schedule a time to meet before the actual investigation date, arrange to meet the client thirty to ninety minutes before the start of the investigation to review and sign the team confidentiality and safety waivers and to tour the site. (See the section "Safety" later in this chapter.) You may even forward your waivers electronically for the client to review before you arrive.

Be methodical and calm—especially in the presence of any clients. They will likely be watching you for any signs of immaturity while you are guests on their property. Listen to what they have to say, and do not feed into any fears or personal theories they may have concerning their perceived haunting. Ask them for the reasons behind their beliefs, and respect their right to own those beliefs. None of us do this work to judge the client or their feelings regarding the situation.

If you plan on utilizing the talents of a trusted medium or clairvoyant, ask the client to withhold any and all information about the property from that person while they work.

Once familiar with the site parameters, establish a "base camp" for your equipment and prepare to conduct your investigation.

Primary Inspection

After interviewing the primary person who has called you in to report the events, you must thoroughly inspect the property to establish a clear understanding of what may have occurred. The first order is to examine every avenue in an attempt to rule out logical explanations for perceived phenomena. An event cannot be classified as true paranormal phenomena until everything naturally occurring has been eliminated.

Should your preliminary inspection find no natural cause for the phenomena and the decision is made to continue with a full investigation, then you should set up all witness interview dates.

Interviewing Witnesses

When taking statements from witnesses, never assume anything. Don't just pull out a notepad or digital recorder. Instead, make them at ease, ask their permission to record the interview, and tell them you want to get what they have to say recorded correctly. Demonstrate that what they have to say is important to you.

Never rush a witness or show any disbelief in what they are saying. Be a good listener.

Never attempt to lead a witness in any direction. Don't assist them by adding words to their statement or writing your own interpretation. Don't offer your opinion. Show interest, create confidence, and encourage them to talk openly.

Interview witnesses separately. First, use a planned list of questions and get those out of the way. Ask them to describe the events in their own words. This will allow them to do most of the talking and elaborate on details the questionnaire may have missed.

If you are going to use a tape recorder during the interview, ensure you know how to operate the device. Conduct a test to ensure proper volume.

Aside from a digital recorder, use a notebook to write down further questions during the interview and note any items that may require additional detail or clarification. Unless the witness begins to veer off topic, don't interrupt the interview. Wait until they have finished speaking, then ask your questions. When asking questions, use plain English; stay away from technical words and jargon, and never discuss information irrelevant to the investigation.

Remember that time is a critical factor, as details will diminish over time. Highlight variations or differences from witness to witness. Keep in mind that most people are not trained observers and therefore see things differently from one another. Most will not remember minor details but rather will focus on the event, and they will normally attach an emotion to it (e.g., sadness or fright).

Encourage the witness to speak only on information that they themselves heard or saw and not information that they have been told about (hearsay).

When there are long pauses and the witness is unsure how to proceed, attempt to ask questions that will require far more than simple yes-or-no answers.

If the witness has a hard time explaining details, they may be able to provide you with a drawing or sketch to help. They may also produce photos. If this occurs, make reference to them on the recording. At a later time, see if you can obtain copies to attach to your report.

If the witness is willing and you have permission, go to the location of the event and conduct the interview there. This may allow them to be more descriptive and will also give you a better insight as to what occurred and where. The surroundings may also stimulate their memory.

Mapping Out the Site

If the client is unable to provide floor plans, draw sketches of the areas under investigation, either on the spot or using photographs. Have someone assist you with room measurements. The floor plan should indicate doors and direction of door swing, windows, forced air vents, and radiator locations. Note air conditioners or fans located in any of the windows and those that are movable or ceiling-mounted. Illustrate hot or cold water piping and lighting locations, including whether there are fixed-wall, ceiling-mounted, or portable lamps. Name the rooms, show stairs, and draw anything of interest (e.g., mirrors). Note the type of floor surfaces (e.g., tile, hardwood, carpet, and so on). When performing a walk through, take your time, inspect areas closely, and become familiar with the location, noting structural changes or modifications that vary from your research.

Daylight Inspection of Target Area

Make every effort to inspect and map the area you intend to investigate during daylight hours. This will allow you to do several important tasks while you have the advantage of bright, natural light.

Map and draw the area if you haven't already, indicating outlets, windows, and furniture placement. Indicate the directions that doors swing, including closet doors. Mark safety hazards; cordon them off with rope or caution tape if necessary.

It is always a good idea to count the windows, especially in old buildings. Start by doing this around the exterior of the building. Note the number. While conducting an interior tour, count them again. The number should be the same. If not, the possibility may be that a hidden room exists. However, keep in mind some exterior windows that exist may have been plastered or drywalled over on the interior during a renovation.

Take control photos and record all of your electronic and atmospheric baseline readings.

Take note of the client's film and book collections for titles associated with paranormal themes. A particular abundance of paranormal media may indicate the client possesses more knowledge and interest in the subject than what they may have expressed.

Note the presence of religious items and icons and any New Age paraphernalia, including smoke cleansing implements, singing bowls, crystals, and spirit boards. Keep in mind that religious beliefs may skew a client's perception of a paranormal event, and New Age accoutrements suggest dabbling in occult rituals (e.g., conjuring, divination, or communication).

Safety

If you are planning to head out on a paranormal investigation, make sure you know and trust the people are going with. Never participate in an investigation with people you don't know, as you can never be sure of their intentions or motives for inviting you. Never conduct an investigation alone. Always let someone in your family know where you are going and when you are to return home. If you know you will miss the return time, call to advise that you are well, then establish a secondary return time.

Lock your vehicle when on an investigation and keep a close watch over your equipment, supplies, and command area.

Make sure you are familiar with the location; know what is around the property you will be working on. This not only helps you understand and identify specific sounds and traffic you may have to deal with, but it also allows you to know if any threats exist in the area. It is also important to conduct a walk through of the property in daylight hours for hazard identification, including open holes or wells on the property, broken glass, old barbed wire, broken fences, boards with nails in them, rotten stairs, floors that may be unsafe, and so on. When entering old structures, make sure there are other exit points.

Look for signs that the location may have been used by gangs, parties, or the unhoused. Also look to see if animals might be nesting in areas inside the dwelling. Always examine the situation carefully and determine whether it is dangerous; if it is, then don't proceed.

Do not enter flooded areas or wet buildings if the power is on; water conducts electricity. If using extension cords, be sure not to lay them through flooded basements or puddles. Don't assume that water-damaged structures are safe. Dry rot could have weakened floor joists, leaving floors unstable.

If you notice a chemical odor, leave the area. Avoid skin contact with contaminated materials or contaminated water.

Always check door handles from both sides of the door. Some hardware works independently from each other; turning one side of a door handle doesn't mean the opposite side will also turn.

There is important safety equipment you should always carry, including your cellular phone. Though all cell phones must be deactivated or set to Airplane Mode while exploring the jobsite (to avoid false positive EMF readings), ensure they are fully charged, and remember that in an accident, they may be your only lifeline. Bring a small first aid kit. Always bring several flashlights with extra batteries. Picture yourself in a large location in the middle of the night without any electricity and your flashlight fails. Now imagine trying to find your way out.

While investigating, use the buddy system, but also be aware when going into basements, tunnels, or other confined areas that doors can close behind you, and if you and your team are all in the same area at the same time, you may become trapped. Always have an exit plan.

Never wander off. Your teammates might not know what happened to you and think you are hurt. Always keep a clear line of communications with your team. Let them know where you are and what you are doing, just as you should always know where they are.

Sleep deprivation is a serious phenomenon. Injuries happen more often when one is tired, as your focus and ability to plan movements are reduced. Not paying attention to commonsense safety issues can put you at risk.

Never use open flames, such as candles or matches, on investigations. Also, if you or team members smoke, do so outside and in a designated area, using a fireproof container to collect the cigarette butts.

Always leave the building as you found it. Don't cause damage. Be professional and respectful and take your garbage with you.

Health Risks

It is important to understand the health risks you may encounter when entering an old building that hasn't been maintained, and what you can do to mitigate them.

Many building materials, furniture, and other items that stay wet for more than a few days will grow mold. Mold releases tiny spores, which can unleash toxins and other cells into the air that can cause allergic reactions and illness. Exposure comes when you move or disturb materials that are moldy. Wear rubber gloves and a dust mask or respirator to reduce your exposure to mold. Look for a mask with an N95 rating. Once used, dispose of the mask and gloves; don't save and reuse these items.

Be aware of possible combustible or explosive gases. Explosive gas vapors can be present in many buildings and may accumulate from decaying materials. Again, if you detect a chemical odor, leave the area.

Identify asbestos-containing products, which may be part of debris. These may include asbestos-cement corrugated sheet, asbestos-cement flat sheet, asbestos pipeline wrap, roofing felt, vinyl-asbestos floor tile, asbestos-cement shingle, millboard, asbestos-cement pipe, and vermiculite attic insulation. All structures (both residential and commercial) built in North America before 1975 may contain significant amounts of asbestos.

Lead is a highly toxic metal that produces a range of adverse health effects. Many homes built before 1978 may contain lead-based paint. Disturbance of materials containing lead-based paint may result in elevated concentrations of lead dust in the air.

Engaging Law Enforcement

After gaining permission to investigate a site, build a good working relationship with the local police. This is very important, especially if you will be active on vacant properties. Let them know the dates and times you will be working on the property and explain your investigation process. Show them you have permission, give them the owners' names, and provide them your contact information if they ask. Most law enforcement officers will appreciate this information, as they won't respond to calls concerning suspicious lights and activity on that property, which would withhold assets from potential crimes occurring elsewhere. Sometimes an officer may come out to see what you are doing. Should they wish to enter the reputed haunted location, politely explain that they (or anyone else) will not be welcome while carrying a firearm.

Chapter 5
INVESTIGATION

We're finally ready to conduct our investigation. The equipment is tested and ready; the team is available, well rested, and prepared to conduct themselves appropriately; and the client is anxiously looking forward to the hours ahead. What will happen next?

Investigation Protocol

The following sections detail the steps necessary to determine the legitimacy of an alleged haunting. As a rule of thumb, it is best practice to investigate a property without any preconceptions or expectations of that property, meaning that the investigative team and mediums should not know the history or reported activity of the location going in. This can be difficult, as normally something from that location drew you to investigate it. It should be the lead investigator, who acquired the contact information, interviewed witnesses, and brought the team on site, who holds that information exclusively. Though the location manager will likely have limited knowledge of the jobsite, the lead is responsible for keeping all information gained prior to taking the job absolutely secret until such time when it is appropriate to share with the investigative team. Doing so prematurely only builds expectations, which, of course, could lead to making things happen to fulfill those expectations.

Information should only be shared with other team members for safety or operational needs. Even then, the information should be extremely limited.

Set up a good quality audio and video surveillance camera(s) and have everyone depart the area. Leaving the place in the best controlled condition possible will help determine if the location is haunted in the shortest amount of time, in most cases. The recording systems can be left for up to several hours, and the data should be analyzed as soon as possible for any captured paranormal activity.

Phase 1

Deploy audio and video surveillance systems in high-traffic areas, such as hallways and main stairways, and in any known hot spots within the dwelling immediately. The camera system should be of high-quality infrared or full-spectrum imaging, with high-definition omni directional microphones with a 15 Hz response.

These systems should be operated for up to six hours of recording, half the time as investigators conduct investigations and half the time with everyone clear of the building, leaving the dwelling empty and silent.

If you are moving around with your recorder, it's extremely important to note the time of day as much as possible (fifteen- to twenty-minute intervals should suffice). Doing so will assist with data corroboration between recording devices, accurately log where the investigators are in relation to each other throughout the duration of the investigation, possibly confirm and corroborate witness experiences, and help to establish a pattern to determine or theorize a possible window of time wherein paranormal activity occurs the most frequently.

Careful review of both the visual and the audio portions should be conducted. Look for anomalies or activity. (See "Recording and Writing Reports" in chapter 6.)

If you are successful capturing anomalous data, utilize the same camera or recording systems in the same locations when conducting follow-up investigations at the site. Experiment further by introducing respectful EVP-provoking methods in tandem with the recording equipment present.

If post-investigation analysis suggests that absolutely no unexplained data was captured in any given area of the site, you may wish to reassess your equipment dispersal plans during successive investigations. You could try using the same camera or recorder one more time or perhaps change up the choice of recording device. Remember that not every investigative visit will be fruitful in terms of acquiring promising results. Sometimes it will take two or three attempts to determine whether spirit people are indeed present, let alone willing to communicate.

Whether it takes one or several visits to the site to acquire compelling data (e.g., audio recordings of phantom-issued names, dates, or conversations or video evidence), it will be up to the lead investigator to decide when to proceed to phase 2 of the site research.

Phase 2

Phase 2 involves the use of pre-tested and trustworthy mediums, and two mediums, if available, are best for this exercise. Mediums should be used separately; they should not be permitted to communicate with (or risk influencing) each other for any reason. The medium present is to be used as a tool like any other piece of data-collecting equipment. No information regarding the history of the location, reports of activity, or EVP results should be shared with the mediums.

Take one medium on a thorough tour of the research site; they should be equipped with a digital recorder (or followed by a team member with a recorder) to ensure everything they report is logged. A second medium can then be introduced to the property separately and also recorded for the duration of their visit.

Phase 3
During phase 3, the research team needs to analyze every piece of data and look for similarities or exact duplication of information between EVP results and the mediums' reports.

This process of surveillance, EVP recording, and alternating between mediums could go on for many visits before there is enough information to make a good comparison.

Phase 4
Phase 4 involves historical research and eyewitness testimony. The investigators should collect all available information from witnesses and historic files related to the location.

Phase 5
All data is scrutinized at phase 5, with investigators looking for relevant data and corroboration between captured EVP, medium reports, witness testimony, and historic research.

For example, if an EVP recording states there is someone named John present, and medium one says they detected a "John," and medium two feels a "John" is there, and history tells you someone named John owned the property in the past, this could be evidence that the spirit of John is haunting the building.

Dead Silence Protocol

A specifically designed operational protocol known as Dead Silence should be used during your investigation. Based on conformity experimentation conducted by Solomon Eliot Asch (1907–1996), this protocol was designed and developed to mitigate the corruption of data collected during an investigation.

Solomon Asch was a Polish American psychologist and pioneer in social psychology. Asch conducted experiments to discover the role social pressure might play in group conformity.[15] Asch found that the majority of people who had participated in the experiments succumbed to social pressure and conformed to specific thoughts or ideas, even though most would later report that they did not really believe what they had been told but had agreed to stand by what they were told in fear of being ridiculed or considered outcasts from the group.

The issue, in terms of investigating a haunting, is that subjective evidence is personal information that cannot be evaluated. In this instance, it is usually a reported experience without other witnesses, and that information can only be accepted or rejected. Following this protocol will not completely resolve this type of experience; however, in some cases, it will provide recorded testimony of the same incident from other witnesses.

The following situations influence witness testimonies, which, in turn, will affect your team's investigation conclusions:

> *Group conformity:* This takes place when an individual
> has the ability to influence and persuade a larger group to
> cooperate in working toward a common goal. This can lead
> to conformity of views, creating a phenomenon known as

....
15. McLeod, "Solomon Asch Conformity Line Experiment Study."

groupthink. In such cases, views relating to the subject are adopted without question, which causes a lack of critical thinking and an automatic rejection of any outside criticism.

Social influence: This may occur when people do not have the answers to questions regarding a situation. This will cause them to lack confidence in their ability to move beyond the situation and seek out better information. When they receive an answer, be it true or false, it is accepted as true.

Emotional contagion: This phenomenon occurs when one person's emotions and behaviors activate similar emotions and behaviors in other people, either consciously or unconsciously. This includes the emotion of fear. Fear expressed by others can elicit fear in ourselves and vice versa.

All too often, when one team member experiences something alarming, they will ask aloud, "Did you see/hear that?" This begins a conversation, which has a tendency to conclude with other team members agreeing with certainty that they had all experienced the same anomaly—even when that wasn't the case. More times than not, investigators will try to fit their experiences into the mold of historical accounts, reported phenomena, and general theory of an active location.

To remove the influences of group conformity, emotional contagion, and social influences, thus providing better, controlled results during an investigation, investigators and observers alike must not communicate with each other, even if they are working side by side. Rather, when something unexplained does occur in the course of the investigation, they are to note the time and location and detail what they believe they experienced.

If the time logs are accurate, the result will be multiple experiences observed by independent individuals in specific locations without influence of any kind. This injects a strong level of credibility to observed events.

How to Employ Mediums Effectively

As mentioned previously, information on location, history, clients, events, or investigation data must never be shared with the medium(s) you decide to include during your investigation.

Ideally, the investigative team should have an individual held in reserve who is not part of the team but rather a trusted outsider. This individual will not be furnished with any investigation-related information whatsoever, with the exception of the location. This individual's task will be to collect the medium and deliver them to the site. Upon arrival, they are to escort the medium throughout the location, recording everything they say.

This individual's lack of knowledge about the client, location's history, or recent events will ensure that the medium is not telepathically reading the person but rather the location itself.

If an individual cannot help with this process, meet your medium away from the investigation site and escort them to it personally. This will help lend even more credibility to your investigation and validity in the minds of skeptics.

Conducting an EVP Session

The preparation for an EVP session is much like that of a Victorian séance. Gather your participants (team members and clients alike) in an area or room that is as quiet and as far removed from outside noise contamination as possible. Have the participants settle comfortably so they are not moving their clothing, shifting, or pacing the floor during the session. Establish beforehand who will ask questions aloud and explain that at least seven to ten seconds of silence must be observed between each question or statement.

Utilize a minimum of two pieces of recording equipment, be they video cameras, digital or analogue recorders, or a combination. Thrill-seekers will not have the patience for this, especially since it means doubling the analysis efforts later. What they may not appreciate is that two or more recording sources that corroborate an anomalous audio "hit" is a far more impressive result than one caught by only a single recorder. Alternately, it is not uncommon for one recorder to capture an anomaly that another one will miss entirely.

Hopefully, when your team entered the investigation site, everyone behaved politely and demonstrated respect for the property leading up to your EVP session(s). Doing so is not only standard practice for a professional team, but having a positive relationship established with your invisible hosts will go a long way toward gleaning recorded results.

Still, it doesn't hurt to reinforce your respectful intentions at the outset of your EVP session. Introduce the team members and explain what it is that you are about to do, what you hope to achieve (i.e., auditory responses), and why you're officiating a meeting.

After introductions and intents are shared, the bulk of the session can begin. Some example questions and statements may include:

+ We're here in your lovely home, hoping to speak with you. We've brought a couple of devices that will help us hear you [indicate the recorders/video cameras], so if you wouldn't mind speaking into them or speaking as loudly as possible, we'd appreciate that a lot.

+ Since it's hard for us to hear you, we'll ask you questions and pause to give you time to answer. When we listen back to our devices, hopefully we'll hear you. Do you understand what I'm saying?
+ Thank you, if you've replied. We're having trouble seeing you, too, so if you don't mind me asking, how many people are here in spirit?
+ I realize this may sound like an odd question, but are you able to share what the current year is with us, please?
+ Are you in a position to share why you've chosen to remain here in spirit?
+ What year did your physical body pass away?
+ If you're not alone, would you tell us the full names of other spirit people that are present so we may address them properly, please?
+ We're here because we're curious about life from your perspective. Are there rules you must abide by where you are? If so, who makes the rules? Can you tell us, please?

As a reminder, try not to dwell on small talk. Prepare questions calculated to give you verifiable replies: names, dates, events, places. Ask probing questions about their existence, including how they perceive the world, how they travel, what their limitations are, and who might police them. These pieces are not only the stuff of credibility to the outside world but important data for our ongoing research into life-after-life phenomena.

The fickleness and unpredictability of ghosts is identical to that of any living person. There may be one or two spirit people present who are eager to communicate, and your initial introductory EVP sessions may garner results straightaway. Conversely, if there are spirit people present who are extremely wary of your presence and are shy or would rather hide by remaining quiet, they will (unless of course your surveillance equipment records them conversing while you are away). In this case, it may simply be a matter of them observing you spending time in their space before they'll be comfortable enough to open up, even a little.

Another rationale is that no one in spirit is present, and as frustrating as this is, you must be prepared for this possibility, too.

You can test this latter quandary by performing multiple EVP sessions at different hours during the investigation. There may be certain points during a ghost's day when they are more likely to be active in terms of manifesting themselves than others. (Some investigators correlate effective results with moon phases, sunspot activity, and natural earth EMF emissions.) An EVP session at four in the afternoon may not be as effective as one at eight at night or even two in the morning (traditionally regarded as part of the witching hour period).

As you investigate more at any given location, you may find yourself needing to experiment by introducing extra elements to your EVP sessions. After all, the name of the game is finding what is most effective at extracting replies. Some suggestions:

- Incorporate a pendulum (but be prepared for yes or no replies only).
- Play some gentle era-appropriate music softly (away from the recorder so the sensitive microphone is not overwhelmed and misses potential EVP responses).
- Offer easily mobile trigger objects to interact with. Place them a few yards away from the nearest investigator (e.g., balls, toy cars, a bell, wind chimes, a meaningful photograph propped upward, an open book).

- Incorporate a proximity device (e.g., REM pod or Mel meter).
- Have someone listening to the session use a parabolic microphone.

If you integrate different elements into your EVP sessions, try not to get distracted by the novelty of these items. Unless the spirit is that of a child, no one with an ounce of dignity wants to be regarded as a performing monkey. Even a child will grow bored of activating lights or alarms after a while. Politely encourage your ghostly hosts to do their best to speak loud enough that your recording devices will hear them, regardless of the items you offer.

Dealing with Uncooperative Spirits

When investigating dwellings, you may run into several complications while attempting to establish communications with the haunter. One of these may be either hesitation or a complete lack of communication.

In cases of hauntings TSG has dealt with, 80 percent of the time, spirits will try to avoid the investigators. For example, if you set your command center up in the living room, they will move to the kitchen. If you move into the kitchen, they might head down into the basement, and so on. They will be where you are not.

Another problem might be that there is a dominant spirit present that will not permit the others to communicate with you, for whatever reason.

Both of these situations are common, and we have developed special methods to employ when dealing with these obstacles:

Squeezing

Squeezing is a technique used to corner a spirit. The challenge for the investigative team is that it must have the resources available to implement this approach. Put one investigator in each room, including basements, attics, hallways, restrooms, pantries, and storage rooms. Equip each investigator with a digital recorder and coordinate so that each investigator asks the same series of questions of the spirits, simultaneously. Because spirits are attached to their dwelling, it is extremely unlikely they will exit the property. The number of people (whose occupancy ensures there is nowhere on the site for spirits to hide), combined with the repetitive nature of their questions, is sure to overwhelm uncooperative spirits and evoke responses that can be recorded.

This method may sound unkind, but in cases where help for the client is needed, the investigators must open a meaningful dialogue somehow. By employing the squeezing technique, the message sent to the normally unresponsive spirit should be this: Cooperate or risk enduring the squeeze repeatedly until you do.

Divide and Conquer

In the case of hesitation or complete lack of communication due to a dominant spirit holding others silent, the investigators must set up two communication sessions simultaneously in the farthest points from each other within the dwelling or property. It is rare that the dominant spirit will be able to control both locations at the same time and so will have to choose one of the two, leaving the other team open for communication.

Haunted Objects and How to Utilize Them

People have a tendency to fall in love with personal possessions and objects, becoming emotionally attached to material things. Such objects could be anything from a religious icon or a piece of artwork to a family heirloom or even a vehicle. Sometimes the love for these objects may run deeper than love for another person. The individual will possess it, defend it with their life, and boast about it.

It may be no wonder that in death they return to attach themselves to these objects. These objects can become home base for haunting activity wherever they are stored, and violent, harmful activity may occur when the object is neglected or shown disrespect in some way.

This also happens with places, not objects, as people develop strong attachments to a home, place of business, or other significant location.

Haunted objects are physical articles that many students of the paranormal believe play host to spirit energy attachment. This would mean that no matter where the object is, it would essentially be that spirit's base of operation. This would imply that no matter what the spirit did or where it went, it would return to the object eventually. If a haunted object exists within a dwelling and can be found and confirmed, then the removal of that object may end the haunting.

Although there are numerous reports of haunted objects, very little evidence has been gathered to support this phenomenon.

Having said this, smaller haunted objects, if truly haunted, provide a unique opportunity in paranormal study, as these objects can be placed in a controlled environment, observed, measured, and scientifically studied. This presents the greatest opportunity to gain verifiable evidence of the afterlife, which leads us to question the validity of many of the popular haunted objects offered up by paranormal collectors and paranormal museums around the globe.

Verification of a Haunted Object

To assess the validity of a haunted object, secure the item in the best controllable location you can find, ensuring control over outside sounds, sunlight, and vibrations. The location should be checked for any baseline electromagnetic and static fields prior to the introduction and placement of the object.

Deploy twenty-four-hour video surveillance, monitoring for movement, light phenomena, sounds, or EVPs. Even though the space is considered sound-controlled, be aware of the possibility that external sounds could still find their way onto your recordings.

Monitor for static field and EMF fluctuations above your baseline data.

Employ motion detectors and geophone device(s) to monitor movement. Be aware that geological activity or even heavy trucks and construction could provide false positives.

To escalate this inquiry, the investigator might consider introducing religious music to the space the allegedly haunted object occupies. The source of the music should remain in the view of your surveillance camera along with the "haunted" object. Play back the music at a low volume in case unknown sounds or EVPs occur and are recorded over the duration of this test.

Record any changes or data. Over time, this could prove that the object in question is truly haunted.

Chapter 6
DATA ANALYSIS

With the laborious task of arranging and executing a full-scale paranormal investigation behind you and the team, there is little time to waste. Every scrap of data that was logged during your time at the research site must now be reviewed and analyzed with as much scrutiny and care as possible.

Analyzing Photos and Video

On the surface, reviewing visual material seems like it should take the least amount of time to complete—particularly still photographs. Still, your analysis of every recording medium used to document your investigation must be extremely thorough and reviewed by other members of the team to ensure accuracy and, ultimately, credibility in the long term. Let's begin with the most straightforward data: the still photograph.

Photo Analysis

Upload your investigation photographs to a reliable storage device (e.g., a quality USB drive or solid-state hard drive) and set your camera(s) aside. Do NOT delete the photographs from the camera at this time. Remove the SD card from the camera and store it in a safe place for later.

View your photographs on a high-quality computer monitor (as opposed to the camera's view screen or a cellphone screen) so that every bit of detail is (hopefully) discernible and sharp.

If the time code function on the camera was not set to imprint the date and time on each photo taken, be sure to note the research location and the approximate time the sequence of photographs was taken for each separate location. Ideally, someone remarked on you taking photographs for the audio device, so you may be able to corroborate the photo-taking actions more precisely during audio review.

Carefully scour each photograph in each sequence, looking for changes between images that may not be immediately accounted for. Be wary of anomalies such as "orbs" (caused by insects, dust, or moisture particles) or streaks of light that might be due to outside traffic or a reflective surface of an object in the room (e.g., a mirror or beveled picture frame glass). Keep in mind that a camera strap may have swung before the camera lens or someone's breath could have been captured (in low-temperature settings), creating images of supposed vortexes or misty shapes, respectively. Image pixelation may also occur, creating questionable blobs or blocks of dark color in high-contrast situations.

Be sure to note instances when photos were taken immediately after communication attempts were made—especially if visual anomalies appear as a possible result!

Since you are viewing copies of original images, feel free to view photos through image software, such as Photoshop or Krita, to brighten pictures taken in low light settings, alter hue or saturation levels, or even convert a color photo to black and white. Save copies of anomaly photos found using the software and note the steps you took to alter the image for future reference.

Video Analysis

No matter whether your video recordings are saved to an SD card or a recordable DVD, be sure to review them using a high-definition monitor and sound system. As audio-video technology is constantly improving, both high-quality monitors and speakers should be available to the modern researcher.

We are going to presume that most video recordings will also include audio recordings made in synch with the images captured, though some investigators do utilize multicamera systems that involve cameras without microphones, likely for reasons of affordability. While audio recorders should ideally be left in the investigation areas where these cameras are positioned and running, extra care is then required to review the separate audio track synchronized with the video picture.

The job of a surveillance video analyst is arguably the most labor-intensive position a team member can undertake. Not only must one keep an extremely careful watch of the movements (or nonmovements) of the area the camera is focused upon, but they must also divide their attention to include listening for audio anomalies.

Whether your team analyzes surveillance footage through a computer while wearing noise-canceling headphones or on a high-definition television system with the volume cranked up, your attention must be glued to that screen the entire time the file is running.

This is a lot to ask, of course, and there is a natural tendency to "drift" and look away from the screen, especially when the area of study is devoid of the living and the ambient hum of the audio becomes a flat, sleep-inducing droning sound. To combat this, pace yourself and analyze footage in ten- or twenty-minute segments, taking frequent breaks so that your eyes, ears, and brain are alert and ready to review the footage that follows. Concentration is key.

Ideally, a time code has been "burned" into the video image. This way, when you are noting the movements and actions of the team as well as any curious visual and audible anomalies, you'll have reference points for not only where to focus on the video file but also the time of day when these occurrences took place. If your camera equipment does not include a time code option, be sure to note the points along the video counter when an investigator has logged the time of day aloud for the benefit of the camera watching them.

Putting It Together

The ultimate goal is to recreate the investigation experience by piecing each visual and audio recording together. Discovering patterns of visual and audible anomalies over the course of several investigations may lead your team to theories and conclusions that suggest who (or what) it is that is responsible for them.

After reviewing both still and video images, determining where you think you've captured anomalies, assemble your observations and share them with other members of the team in a peer review process (see "Peer Review" later in this chapter). In the event that you have captured something strongly resembling paranormal evidence, ensure that the SD card(s) containing the original metadata are no longer to be used and will be stored and filed safely for future reference. These cards may be needed for deeper professional analysis by a skeptical third party.

Case Research

Years ago, when people wanted to do research, they had two basic options to explore: talk with experts in the field or visit the nearest library and locate the information required.

In 1998, with the launch of Google, all that changed. The problem we now face is poor research discipline. By taking the easy route using a search engine, we have the ability to find information faster and without much effort. However, the internet contains billions of posts by millions of people who can virtually share anything they want. Conflicting data, one-sided agendas, and cherry-picked information are plentiful. Without due diligence, it is easy to discover information that corresponds to what you want while bypassing data that conflicts with your ideas. While this could happen in the past as well, it was nowhere near the epidemic proportions we see today. This problem is aggravated further by the proliferation of self-published books released without fact checks, legal examination, or contextual verification.

When researching a subject, all avenues of information should be explored. Cross-checking several verifiable sources to ensure the data is valid will strengthen your final report. Remember that the conclusions you reach will reflect your reputation as a sensible, credible investigator.

Beware of articles or posts that boast survey or statistical data without revealing the sources or the exact information collected and the context in which questions were asked. Be cautious of self-proclaimed experts.

Historical Research

One of the most important things an investigator will do is conduct historical research into the property they are investigating. This will provide information that may verify some of the data collected during your time on the property. It will allow you to visualize a larger picture of who once lived there, what the building may have looked like originally, its uses through time, changes to the structure, and any major events that took place there.

Most investigators will conduct their investigations first and then research the history of a property last. This allows the investigators to compare historical data to the various information collected through EVPs, mediums, and so on. This method is mostly preferred because by looking into the history last, it cannot influence your investigation by offering expectations and preconceived theories about the property. When performing historical research, an investigator looks for events that have occurred in the past that may suggest a reason for a haunting to take place on the property under scrutiny.

Sidenote: While this method is great for specific hauntings, be alert to the danger of altering one's field results to fit an historical narrative (a regrettable trend of many paranormal TV shows).

On the property, check basements and attics, recalling that many older buildings used newspapers as insulation. Any newspaper found can give you very specific dates.

Talk to the owner and learn what they know about the building. See if there have been any major renovations done. Ask after the existence of any exterior outbuildings that may have been razed (e.g., sheds or barns), especially if working in a rural location.

Talk to neighbors who have resided in the area for a long period; they may have information on the property and events related to the site.

Deeds are extremely important, as they will start you on the path to establishing a chain-of-title search, which will tell you a great deal of information, such as owners' names, value of property, usage, and even construction and renovation information, site surveys, and plans. Work backward from the current deed to previous owners.

Local archives will retain fire insurance plans. These documents will hold information about the neighborhood, lot, and address numbers, which is very important, as sometimes street names and numbers can change over history. A fire insurance plan can illustrate the size and position of the building you are investigating on the lot in relation to other buildings and roads. It can also provide information on building materials, building type, and usage.

Assessment rolls originated for taxation purposes. There can be a great deal of information found in these documents, including information on ownership and a detailed description of the property and any buildings. Assessment rolls are usually accessible through municipal city halls.

Census records are useful for determining property ownership and owners' occupation, family members, boarders, tenants, employees, and their respective ages. Due to privacy laws, these records are only released publicly about a hundred years or so after the original date. Today, most are viewable from around 1920 and before.

Old city directories are handy, especially if the street name has not changed. They can give you previous resident names. By following the names through these directories, you can get an idea of how long specific people resided in the building or at the location you are investigating.

Building permits are usually available at the local city hall. They are normally maintained on microfilm and contain information about property owners, value of a building, architects, and building usage.

Aerial photographs can give you a larger view of the property you are investigating and may show you important changes over the years. These are normally kept by the municipal archives.

Maps can provide you with an overview of the property and its neighborhood, parish, township, village, and any land title plans.

Other archive records may hold reports, files, and old photographs of the neighborhood and possibly the building you are investigating.

A veritable gold mine of information awaits you at local historical societies. They hold enormous volumes of information on the area, including neighborhoods and residences. Be prepared to leave a donation or pay a small fee for the services rendered by passionate historians, who will likely be all too pleased to help.

You may be able to access a great many birth, death, and marriage records online or through the local municipality. Other sources worth consulting are local church and parish records and genealogical societies and websites.

If you have specific details such as an address and people's names, newspapers are a great way to collect information on events such as weddings, engagements, births, deaths, accidents, murders, fires, and so on. In some cases, articles covering social gatherings may list your subject's name as an attendee. Noting local and world events surrounding the lifetime of your subjects may inspire a line of questioning that might evoke a response at the investigation site later.

In the digital age, library services have become a sadly underutilized resource. They provide a wealth and wide range of local information including books, microfilm, microfiche, county or municipal atlases, old photos, maps, neighborhood plans, and local information on past events, free of charge. Some libraries may house historical society materials, including journals and rare, locally produced publications that mention news of interest connected to the investigation site or its neighbors.

Local cemeteries can provide information on people who lived in the community along with birth and death information.

Although social media sites like X (formerly Twitter), Facebook, and even YouTube are not good sources of research information on their own, they can still play a useful part. Using such social media sources to connect with a former owner or tenant of a property under investigation could be helpful. Locating historical entries or blogs on people and property could lead you to people or reports related to your subject matter, making these people easier to connect with, and may possibly verify information you already have. Scan the comments content for additional leads. A platform participant may have been inspired to share their own information pertaining to the site in question.

Many businesses operate specialized archives pertaining to the company business or historical property they own or operate. Check your local directory for local museums and historical groups. Some municipalities operate a museum or police or criminal archive. Military service member legions can be a valuable resource for information regarding buildings that may have been used during wartime.

A Word on Historians

In the course of your work, you may meet well-meaning, locally based historians eager for opportunities to share their knowledge and contribute to your research into an alleged haunting. Many of these people have developed a serious handicraft from what was once a personal hobby and are called upon by heritage preservation societies to conduct public presentations from time to time. Some extroverted historians host walking tours for profit or charity. The Searcher Group has the utmost respect for these impassioned living bastions of historical knowledge, and we appreciate their efforts to keep long-forgotten eras of time relevant—more than they will ever know.

That said, as investigators collecting facts, we must take into consideration that these same historians are also human and that human memory is fallible. Likewise, storytelling is also extremely prone to embellishment. Personal opinion, imagination, and oft-repeated legend and lore often blurs or obscures pure fact. The average paying tourist likely doesn't care whether what they are being told on a historical walking tour has been embellished or not. After all, most simply wish to be entertained first, educated second.

This is not to say independent historians are completely unreliable people. Far from it. What we suggest here is that your team use their statements of fact as launchpads to begin your own deep dive into research using the previously mentioned authorities. Don't be afraid to ask a historian for their source materials. Forthright historians will admit to stories that are based on lore or hearsay. Like us, you too may uncover historical fact that completely alters or even debunks what you've been told. Open-minded historians may appreciate being updated or corrected. Others may feel bent out of shape having their expertise questioned. The bottom line is *your* concern—that you have some serious work to corroborate.

Peer Review

You have spent many hours carefully analyzing photographs, video footage, and audio recordings. Now one of the last steps to complete before a final report is ready to file is to corroborate what you think you've found with your teammates.

It should come as no surprise that the Dead Silence protocol (see chapter 5) applies at this stage, too. Once you feel you've narrowed down some interesting anomalies, prepare to share them with your peers without revealing what you think you're seeing or hearing. Similar to bringing a medium on site, you can't risk influencing anyone else's interpretation of the possible evidence you have captured by giving them your perceptions ahead of their own.

Set up an analysis meeting with the team and share the materials you wish to confirm. Encourage everyone in attendance to write their impressions before disclosing what it is you think you're seeing or hearing, then compare your perceptions with those of the team. The team members should then share their materials with you in a similar manner.

If an in-person meeting is not possible, share the appropriate image or audio files electronically. Again, do this without including your interpretative comments. In the case of audio files, it is acceptable to share the time code information of the suspected sound anomaly so that your teammates can skip straight to the relevant analysis cues, but we can't stress this enough: Do not share what you think you've heard before your peers have logged their interpretations.

If you are a sucker for punishment and boast particularly keen auricular skills, after you've logged your impressions of the specific anomalies that have been shared with you, feel free to listen to your teammates' entire audio files for yourself and log anything else that comes into question. Our team members do this with each others' audio files and have sometimes caught EVPs they missed completely, either due to human error (e.g., tiredness, personal biases, mis-interpretations) or differences in audio playback technology (e.g., sound card or headphone quality).

Should differing opinions emerge regarding a particular anomaly, include both (or all) of them in the final report. Not all interpretations are conclusive. Those that are can be safely classified as verified EVPs or visual aberrations.

Be forthright with your client about multiple interpretations. By admitting you cannot say with absolute certainty what you have captured, you and the team will garner significantly more outside respect and credibility than if you commit to a single, unalterable interpretation and are challenged on it later (and likely publicly).

Recording and Writing Reports

The following protocol applies primarily to audio recordings and the audio recorded by video camera systems. Video phenomena is important, but the environment at the time phenomena occurs is detailed and recorded or imprinted visually for convenient playback. If your team cannot afford to subject every room or space on site to camera systems or team members to monitor them, audio recorders become one's primary source of logging paranormal phenomena.

As such, it is up to *you* to detail and account for as many elements of your investigation as possible. With practice and experience, you will be glad you logged something as inane and normal as a neighborhood dog barking a few seconds before a disembodied crash sound was recorded that was not heard with the naked ear.

Common environmental sounds, such as a dog barking, act as data markers we can use to corroborate our findings with other devices that may have also logged unexplainable data. Let's say you record the dog barking outside while you're investigating the attic of a house. When you listen back to that recording, you note that seven seconds after the last bark, a loud crash occurred that you didn't hear at the time of the recording. A surveillance camera was in operation in a room directly below you at the same time but was activated a few minutes after you started your audio recorder, so the recorded data between the two devices are not in sync. Presuming the room monitored by the camera was otherwise quiet, you can use the dog bark as a point of reference to discover whether the crash sound was also recorded seven seconds afterward.

This illustrates why it is absolutely imperative that everyone participating in an investigation logs their movements, natural bodily functions, effect on the environment (e.g., creaks, squeaks, thuds, and knocking), observations, and any environmental effects on their well-being as clearly and distinctly (no whispering or murmuring) as humanly possible while being recorded in any capacity.

Presuming you have team members taking photographs of every area under investigation, it doesn't hurt to audibly describe what you observe of your surroundings as you tour the location with your recorders. Log device readings as they change. Include your feelings and state of mind as you explore. You will be able to corroborate what you see with the photo, and you may inadvertently trigger an EVP response by someone in spirit form who wishes to add their comments or corrections to yours.

Data Analysis

When writing papers or reports, keep in mind the differences in the information being presented—which is either quantitative or qualitative research. As a field investigator, your report may contain both types of research, and you should try to distinguish between the two within your report.

Quantitative research is considered to be objective. It uses statistics and the data can be accurately measured. Data collection methods are highly structured and the samples used are large, such as recording patterns in phenomena that follow statistical data. From that data the investigator can formulate facts, theories, and the ability to point out patterns.

Qualitative research is data derived, not measured. It provides observations and descriptions and is subjective. Collection methods are unstructured, and any samples are small. Most of what is normally found during an investigation is qualitative as it is usually based on personal experience, observation, and witness interviews.

Although we dedicate our digital recorders to recording para-normal activity and EVPs, it's a good idea to carry a personal digital recorder to log your observations, experienced feelings, personal experiences, and important notes during the investigation.

We are often asked about our writing process, and a common question is: How do you recall so much detail?

Apart from the frequency of field study opportunities, the answer lies primarily within the time it takes to process the data acquired during an investigation. A serious ghost research organization requires that its participating field members submit reports and testimonials to the team leader(s) immediately following each individual investigation.

Realistically, since we're talking about several hours of data to carefully scrutinize between multiple audio and video recording devices, a twenty-four-hour turnaround for a satisfactory report is not a practical expectation. As our own members have lives with full-time careers and families to consider, a comprehensive analysis of an eight-hour investigation will often take place over the course of a week or two.

Because human memory tends to fade, it is imperative to list as much detail in your reports as possible. By doing so, we can recreate the investigation experience as much as possible with the added bonus of multiple perspectives. Corroboration of the investigators' data is as close to being scientific as we can get.

Writing Your Report

When writing your report, include the location, date, names, and roles of the investigating team members, names of guest investigators, and the names of the location hosts, if they were present.

You may wish to include the weather conditions during the time of the investigation along with the moon phase, geomagnetic activity, humidity level, and so on.

It's a good idea to establish how you intend to label and distinguish probable paranormal phenomena from the body of the material you're about to share. In our case, we flag possible EVPs and significant visual and sound phenomena in italics, which makes locating these anomalies easy to find when scanning through our reports. Any personal thoughts, suggestions, or theories that spring to mind as we analyze our data are underlined. We've included a portion of one of our reports as an example.

GEORGETOWN TOWN HALL
Georgetown, Ontario
June 1, 2024
Team: Peter Roe (lead), Paul Palmisano (sr. surveillance), James McCulloch
Client: Trish Past (Halton Historical Society host), Robert Jonson (custodian)
(Notes in italic indicate likely paranormal or curious phenomena. Notes underlined indicate secondary thoughts, considerations, and items to corroborate and follow up on.)

Log Your Recording Devices
Begin each file analysis with the model name of the device that produced the recording. Include the file name, the length of the file about to be analyzed, and the time of day the recording (audio or video) began. You may also wish to record the time of day the recording ended, but this is not particularly necessary.

OLYMPUS
VN320563 (1:17:34) (19:26 hrs)

00:29 – As Peter logs that a member of the cleaning staff is upstairs, a faint EMI static buzz can be heard under his voice for four seconds.

01:48 – The team follows Trish and walks northward from the front foyer into the former council chambers and settles to listen to the environment while recording.

12:05 – After logging EMF readings are stable and no other observances to report, Trish leads the team upstairs to the greenrooms behind the stage. As James is the last to settle, quietly…

EVP (13:15; older male, faint, annoyed): They're here, now.

13:20 – Peter clears his throat.

EVP (13:22; same male, irritated): Whatcha want? (Corroborate with James's recorder.)

27:54 – With no further occurrences, the team walks into dressing room #1.

Log Your Movements

In the likelihood you will explore many different areas accompanied by your digital recorder, make a point of audibly marking when you enter a room, who is with you, who might enter or exit the room, and when you leave the room.

33:26 – As James asks how much Peter can see himself in the antique mirror, a woman's voice speaks under his voice, resembling, "Other way out, Harper." (This is extremely speculative. Compare with James and surveillance footage around the 19:50 hrs mark.)

34:12 – Trish leaves dressing room #1 to accompany Robert (custodian) downstairs and to secure the doors behind him. They are on the main floor by 36:18, and Trish locks the front entrance at 36:51. Paul exits dressing room #1 at 36:58 and settles in dressing room #2 across the hall shortly afterward.

37:15 – As Trish can be heard ascending the stairs, Paul's gauss meter spikes loudly. Trish quietly settles in dressing room #2 by 37:26, observing Paul following the EMF field.

Log the Time of Day

As mentioned in chapter 5, logging the time of day throughout the course of your investigation will assist with augmenting your final report.

Log EVPs

Be as honest as you can when interpreting possible EVP recordings. In other words, don't conceive inaccurate words to fit a narrative that may be associated with the site you're investigating (that's what your favorite TV investigators do). Many disembodied words or statements are aggravatingly distorted in whole or in part, so after a dozen or so repeat listens, do your best to make sense of the EVP, noting the speaker's gender and age range, demeanor, clarity, if there's an accent, number of syllables, pauses between words, phonetic sounds, and possible alternate interpretations.

> Peter (01:12:51): Well, nobody's, uh … I don't know if anybody's here with me and whether these really weak signals are stray EMF frequencies floating through the room …
>
> *EVP (01:13:09; male, distant, shouting)*: Get 'em! (Very speculative; could also be "Callum!" or even "Git out!")
>
> Peter (01:13:10): I'm sure you can appreciate that after a while it becomes very tiresome and boring for me to speak to the empty air. I hope I'm speaking with somebody.
>
> 01:14:13 – Peter tags the time as 11:03 p.m. (23:03 hrs) and stops this recording.

Once you've logged the points where the possible EVP hits occur in the course of your audio or video recording timeline, ask your teammates to interpret your findings without first telling them what *you* think you're hearing. Don't influence their perception; wait until they've logged their own before comparing interpretations. Their insight may be agreeable, surprise you, or make more sense than yours!

If possible, keep your recorded files between ninety and one hundred and twenty minutes. This will help make the task of deep analysis seem less arduous. Audio-playing software tends to limit the option to scroll back to exact points in the file timeline if the file is too large.

Log Spirit Box Sessions

When transcribing spirit box sessions, be prepared to identify definitive words in a single phrase mixed with garbled, clipped, or dropped words. Don't be afraid to log what you *think* was said but do add a note admitting your perception is speculative. Make note if you have alternate words or phrases to offer.

Describe the gender, age, volume, and attitude of the voice emitted through the spirit box. These details are helpful elements to include in the transcript and will save time in reopening the files to replay the moment.

If there are portions of the spirit box audio that are too clipped, electronic-sounding, or otherwise nonsensical no matter how many times you replay them, don't disregard them but include mention of them in your final report.

Below is a very brief outtake from a particularly fruitful investigation. While it's not necessarily exciting or intriguing, this sample illustrates the amount of detail to document in the hope that clues for your investigation may appear among the seemingly extraneous noise.

24:45 – Settling on the edge of downstage-center, Peter activates the P-SB7 again for a second session. He tags the sweep as FM Reverse. As he observes, the volume is at its peak ("30") and the sweep is whizzing at 100 milliseconds. Nothing but static pounds from the handheld box.

Peter (25:00): Anybody here with us up here?

P-SB7 (25:11; male, static-filled): Hey.

Peter (25:12): Hello.

P-SB7 (25:14; Female, possible British accent): Hello.

Peter (25:15): How are yo—

P-SB7 (25:15): [Loud electronic scratch sound]

Peter (25:16): Who's this?

P-SB7 (25:20; female or child): Oh! (Sounds more like a hiccup with the resonant echo similar to a Ping-Pong ball bounce.)

P-SB7 (25:21): [Electronic-sounding music note]

Peter (25:24): What's your name, please?

P-SB7 (25:27; male, deep voice, static-filled): [Indistinguishable three-syllable statement] (In the vein of "Get away.")

P-SB7 (25:30; same male, static-filled, quiet): Paul. (Very speculative; could also be "Bob.")

Not everything these devices spew is useful. Admitting this lends credibility to you and your team more than making something up to fit a fictional narrative does. Don't give skeptics fuel to demean your work and earnest efforts.

Post-Analysis Conclusion

Once all devices have been analyzed thoroughly and significant occurrences properly flagged, send your report to the investigation team leader. This person will gather everyone's analysis, try to find matching events that corroborate each other between different devices, and analyze the raw data to confirm and assess the evidence for themselves. A team meeting may be called for the express purpose of evidence review to fine-tune the conclusions of the analysis.

Client Report Compilation

From this point, the team leader collates every piece of team information into a final report for the client that describes the investigation and its findings as clearly and unsensationally as possible. Avoid emotional language, abbreviations, and heavy technical language. This report will be presented to the client, and they will most likely not know what an EVP is or what a spirit box does. Depending on the quality or quantity of evidence your team experienced or gathered, keeping one's excitement in check may be challenging, but as your client is looking to you to take their reaction cues from, try to maintain a calm demeanor as you share your findings with them in the following order:

Introduction: Describe the process of how you and your team came to learn of the investigation site. Disclose whether the client contacted you directly or you approached the client with a request to conduct work on their property.

Objectives of the investigation/research: Explain the needs of the client, especially if they initiated contact with you and the team. Include what the client hopes to achieve by allowing you time and access to their property and whether there is a sense of urgency to the case. Document whether the client ruled out every physically explainable cause for the activity they (and perhaps others) have perceived before your involvement. Clarify whether the client is seeking a resolution or is simply interested in confirming they have a haunting on their hands.

Methods of investigation/research used: Summarize the timeline spent investigating and researching the property. List only the relevant periods where promising data was captured, describing the situation leading up to the evidence collection. Explain the equipment that was present to capture the evidence (e.g., digital recorder, IR surveillance, Mel meter, powder trap).

Results and conclusions: Following the investigation summary, use this opportunity to break down the evidence that was mentioned by sharing your team's professional opinions regarding each item. Help the client understand that some EVPs were clearer and more definitive than others. Illustrate that a stray image in a photograph, while interesting to look at, may not be considered solid proof but rather inconclusive, perhaps as an example of pareidolia. If your team was impressed with capturing an EVP response at the same time a proximity meter alarmed, do not hesitate to share this.

The longer you work in this field, the more apt you are to experience similar events as you investigate. Be honest and share when you came across similar findings elsewhere (without disclosing the other site's identification, of course). If the perceived haunting at this client's location is not a malevolent one, use your position as a seasoned professional to assure your client, "I have seen this many times before, and experience has shown me that unless something dramatically changes, you shouldn't have a problem…"

When you provide information to your client, don't jump to conclusions or provide wild assumptions. Let them know that what you found is your opinion or best guess and why.

Recommendations: As the professionals your client perceives you are, what you recommend post-investigation carries a lot of weight. If your initial visit came up with partial evidence and was largely inconclusive, politely suggest a follow-up investigation and say why. Perhaps your analysis has inspired an idea for an experiment you'd like to try. Perhaps your evidence was so fruitful you'd like to bring a medium in to corroborate it. If the investigators were thrown around and injured by demonic forces, use this opportunity to recommend reliable outside assistance.

References, historical data, news articles, and so on: While you may wish to pepper all your results and conclusions with specific examples of historical data, here is where including the team's historical research is appropriate. Include data relevant to the site, the neighborhood, or even the community, especially if some sort of disastrous event occurred that may have played a role in the haunting. Accurately cite all the resources for future reference.

Chapter 7
WHAT TO DO WHEN
EVIDENCE GOES VIRAL

Let's say your team has had a particularly successful investigation. Your video cameras captured an event truly remarkable that shouldn't have happened (by science's reckoning) and is downright spooky. You have also recorded indisputable class A EVPs that are direct responses to the investigators' questions, and you can't wait to share news of these captures with the world. There are dozens of internet platforms at your disposal to immediately display your team's good fortune. This is news, after all. We have been there ourselves many times. We understand the rush of excitement when an incredible image or audio response has not only been captured but verified after very careful analysis and dismissal of normal explanations.

Take a step back and be as objective as possible. How wise or beneficial would it be to share your capture with the world just yet? Might doing so affect (or even harm) your ongoing investigation? Will posting your claim amass more criticism and suspicion than praise and (that ever-elusive) respect?

Before deciding on your answer, consider the following real-life experience.

The Circled-Wagon Phenomenon

Several years ago, The Searcher Group was invited to explore the rural property of a small, historic village. During our first visit, Paul managed to capture an unmistakable color image of a young Caucasian male literally thrusting his face toward the camera Paul was holding while he was alone taking a series of photographs inside an otherwise empty barn loft. Paul had no idea he had captured this picture among the series he'd taken until he descended from the loft and began reviewing his camera on the ground floor minutes later. Needless to say, this was an incredibly exciting find and inspired many communication efforts directed toward this young male over the following year in an effort to identify him by name.

Upon the discovery of this image of "Barn Boy" (the team's off-site nickname for the lad), Richard made the purposeful decision *not* to splash it across the internet. After all, we had barely scratched the figurative surface of this investigation; there was likely a lot more information to learn, and inciting a storm of controversy focused on a small, close-knit village community would likely have forced our clients to put an abrupt end to our work efforts.

After eighteen months, we were unable to learn this particular youth's full name using on-site communication attempts (extenuating circumstances were many during this case). We had no alternative but to approach the community for help. You might imagine our anxiety as we walked into the offices of the sole newspaper in the nearest town and asked to speak with a reporter about our story and our incredible find. If someone from the community could positively ID Barn Boy, that photograph would be hailed as definitive proof that ghosts exist the world over.

After hearing us out, the reporter excused himself, returned with the head editor, and asked us to repeat our story. The staff photographer was summoned next, and we transferred the entire sequence of Paul's photographs to his laptop to examine thoroughly. The meeting concluded, and we were advised to wait a few days before we would receive word on proceeding with an article asking for the community's assistance, accompanied by the world's first look into the face of a real ghost.

Sometime between our leaving the newspaper office and Richard's arrival home, a phone call was made, originating from the newspaper to a long-standing resident of the village we were conducting our investigation in. This townsperson then called Richard, aggressively demanding information on the origins of the Barn Boy image and the extent of our knowledge of him.

Paul's photographic find had evidently struck a nerve between the newspaper's head editor and the village resident, who knew each other well. It appeared they had each other's backs, since both of them knew the identity of Barn Boy and neither were willing to divulge it.

A few days later, we received a joint email from the reporter we had initially met with. He informed us that the staff photographer discovered an anomaly while examining the metadata of the sequence of photographs we'd provided. Without directly accusing us of manufacturing the photo, he summarily dismissed us. The story never ran and the team's collective dream of solving two astonishing mysteries at once came crashing down.

Over the ensuing years, a heritage proponent and friend of The Searcher Group ended up working closely with the same village resident, the two of them advocating for the preservation of various historical buildings. Fully aware of the importance of identifying Barn Boy, our friend made several discreet inquiries of the secretive village resident on our behalf, but to no avail. Before she passed away herself, our friend shared that the closest answer she received from the resident was that they did in fact know who Barn Boy was.

The point of imparting this experience relates to what we have dubbed the Circled-Wagon Phenomenon. Any investigator who finds themselves working within a small community—where everyone knows everyone—will likely encounter this for themselves: No matter how honest, respectful, and well intentioned you are, rightly or wrongly, if you didn't grow up there, you will always be considered an outsider and will therefore be perceived as a threat to the residents of that community. Don't expect to receive much help with your case outside of innocuous historical research; in the course of your investigation, you too may stumble upon secrets that some desire remain that way, indefinitely.

In our case, we are left to imagine that we have ourselves a photo of a murdered, missing person whom at least two local people aware of his death can positively identify. Sadly, frustratingly, both will likely take his name with them to their own graves and the world will continue searching for that elusive proof that ghosts exist.

Alternate Means of Sharing

The Searcher Group has been fortunate to work with commercial book publishers who have helped share some of our most notable field experiences. Though some of our findings have concerned highly sensitive subject matter (e.g., sexual assault and murder), our supportive publishers have never treated our discoveries with kid gloves. As such, the true nature of this line of work—and some of its inherent dangers—can be appreciated by nonfiction readers and prospective investigators alike.

Public speaking appearances are another means we use to share our field findings and theories and promote our free services. These events are invaluable ways to connect with communities and sometimes lead to additional research opportunities.

Uploading content to your team website and YouTube and Facebook profiles is obviously another means of sharing amassed field content and, depending on the parameters you establish, can also result in feedback, both positive and negative, from around the globe.

Determining Whether to Share

The Searcher Group has been very careful with what it has shared with the world. We have sat on a number of items for *years* before deciding on a means (and an appropriate time) that would best suit the material. Peter owns very strong audio evidence of activity taking place inside an otherwise deserted tunnel at Fort George, Niagara-on-the-Lake, Ontario, that he wanted to share, but because video evidence garners the *most* attention and his audio captures ran for several minutes at a time, he had no effective way to do so. Years later, Peter realized he could make slideshow videos using still photographs of the study site *and* add a silent commentary using subtitles throughout the segment so as not to distract from the most important feature: the audio evidence.

These videos ("Tunnel Ghosts of Fort George," parts 1 and 2) were released on YouTube in October of 2015 and have since earned a modest number of views despite the absence of visual evidence of a soldier's ghost.

Richard also held back from publicly releasing a piece of surveillance video footage we captured decades ago because the recorded phenomena lasted fifty-four minutes. Considering the insatiable demand for instantaneous information and sound bites in this day and age, how many people would honestly sit and concentrate on a soundless, shape-shifting, disappearing-reappearing swatch of light slowly manifesting at varying intensities and creeping along the length of a hallway wall for fifty-four minutes?

Ultimately, using editing software, the footage was sped up slightly to compress the overall runtime of the video and released on YouTube in late 2015 as "Ghost Activity Caught on Surveillance." Since most "ghost footage" usually lasts a split second, the original runtime of this capture alone is astounding, to say the least. However, because there are no discernible shadow figures walking past the camera, no movement from the doll placed on a chair at the end of the hall, and (gasp!) NO DEMONS appearing, as of March 2025, the video has only amassed 1,045 views.

The team also possesses wintertime surveillance footage of a pair of large, shadowy dogs running together across the snow-covered parking lot of an urban commercial property, barreling through a short, snowy bush, and disappearing headlong into a brick wall behind the shrub. The incident was captured from two different camera angles, and it all happened within the space of a second. If that isn't incredible enough, the animal figures leave no paw prints in the ground snow, yet snow resting on top of the bush falls from the branches as they shake in reaction to the dogs' collision (on their way into the solid brick wall of the building). Despite numerous requests made to the property owner and earnest promises to obscure identifying landmarks, the public will never see this "hellhound" film footage.

Imagine now—in a world under continuous surveillance—how much *more* compelling evidence of paranormal activity has been captured across the planet and subsequently hidden or destroyed by thoughtless corporations before it could be shared and studied.

Dealing with the Media

Let's say your team has made some progress and the field results are undeniably valid and credible. You've shared what is safe to share online for the world to see and your clients are content with this.

Your team may be contacted by a mass media representative curious about you, your team, and the results of your painstaking labors. Outside the month of October, the reporter is likely after a human-interest story, while the weeks leading to Hallowe'en are when most print and video articles manifest en masse, owing to the season and the populace's broader acceptance of ghosts at this time of year. The media format could be a newspaper, print magazine or e-zine article, an evening news clip, or a radio or podcast interview.

As team leader, you may have a member of the team assigned to handle media relations, but if not, it's up to you to utilize opportunities such as these to call attention to the legitimacy of your no-nonsense community service and "sell" your volunteer services without sensationalizing your fieldwork.

Regrettably, extreme scenarios depicted on reality TV have encouraged the audience of paranormal fans to expect a demon to be involved with every haunting, when not long ago, the fact that we would capture direct replies from unseen entities *alone* would make for an exciting story. There's not much we can do about this except be honest about our own findings.

Preparation ahead of media requests is key.

The window of opportunity to fill with information is usually short (often two to five minutes at best), so have some key points ready to share in a cohesive, easy-to-follow way for the audience to absorb and remember.

In the case of print media, don't hesitate to ask the reporter for their questions ahead of the interview. They may send you the questions and base their report around your replies. If they do, take advantage of the opportunity to slip in additional team-promoting information that they may not have expected or thought to have asked for.

During interviews, it helps greatly to convey confidence but not cockiness. Leave the acting to those who lead ghost walks.

For those new to this process, general talking points may include your rank or position within the team, when the team was created, the team's mission statement, and the number of team members at present. It's an opportunity to state that the investigations your team conducts are not like ones seen on TV. While your team uses much of the same equipment, your investigations are conducted calmly, respectfully, and sensitively. Reinforce that any field data that is shared publicly is done so with full written permission from the client.

The Searcher Group also hosts public speaking engagements and fundraising events. It's our way of giving back to the community and a chance to express our gratitude to our clients for allowing us to conduct our research on their properties. If your team hosts a website or offers similar opportunities for the public to meet its members, try to mention your availability within the context of an interview.

Dealing with Reality TV Producers

Once Great Britain's *Most Haunted* hit the airwaves in 2002, the paranormal-themed branch of reality TV was born. Two years later, the exploits of a pair of daytime plumbers and nighttime *Ghost Hunters* from Rhode Island were introduced to North America. Four years after that, a trio of award-winning documentary filmmakers entered the series realm on the Travel Channel in *Ghost Adventures*.

The ratings success of these early pioneers of para-TV has since spawned countless copycats and theme variations across the globe, each formulating new angles that make their series different from what came before.

When controversy surrounding a popular on-screen medium on *Most Haunted* erupted in 2005, the series producers avoided charges of fraud when Britain's Office of Communications declared the show was for entertainment purposes only and should not be viewed as a depiction of serious scientific investigation.

Despite this ruling and the message behind it, an abundance of viewers continue to place their complete faith in the escapades of colorful, often relatable characters who seem capable of solving alleged hauntings within the space of forty-two minutes before moving on to a different location and starting anew.

Members of The Searcher Group are certainly not above watching broadcasts such as these, but having endured some radical experiences ourselves, we view them much more critically than most. Not only do we appreciate the entertainment value they offer, but we recognize that reintroducing the existence of ghosts into the mainstream zeitgeist has reduced the stigma attached to paranormal phenomena somewhat. This has led to laypeople becoming more open to discussing their own experiences with their peers. We would also be remiss to disregard the fact that forward advancements in available field technology would not have happened if some of the engineering minds behind the scenes of *Ghost Adventures* didn't create them for experimental purposes.

The Searcher Group treads an awkward line regarding its work. On one hand, our team does not wish to be associated in any way with commercialized para-pop culture that is widely believed to be real, while on the other, without access to that same media, our means of sharing experiences, advancing theories, and starting a serious discussion with those who are truly interested in facts is extremely limited.

Richard has been approached on several occasions by television producers hoping to feature The Searcher Group in an ongoing series format. Certainly, this would bring the much-needed attention (and funding) the team's work deserves. But because television is a ratings-based medium, the endgame is always the same: The on-screen team must accrue as many scares as possible within a set amount of time and move on to a new location to hold the viewers' interest and keep them tuning in for more.

As any truly serious investigator can attest, this is not the reality of ghost phenomena, and as such, most proposals by TV producers are summarily and politely declined. In our case, the exceptions have involved recreated and extremely condensed adaptations of singular cases (*Overshadows* seen on *A Haunting* and *Northern Mysteries*) and appearances over two seasons of *Evil Encounters* (a.k.a. *Fear the Woods* in America) sharing TSG theory and professional advice in testimonial fashion.

If you, as team leader, are ever approached by a producer whose sole job is to create media content for entertainment purposes, you have an important decision to make: Stick to your ethics and maintain your team's reputation as credible researchers or risk sullying everything you and your professional team have established *and* contribute to the harm professional teams are encountering—all because the lure of potential widespread adoration is greater than anything you *think* you will achieve otherwise.

Another factor to consider is being financially compensated for contributing material to someone else's moneymaking production. While The Searcher Group will never accept payment from clients for its services, we insist on compensation from people and organizations looking to profit from *our* hard work. It's astonishing to consider how many producers have turned away from us at the thought of actually paying *us* to provide *them* with media content that they will profit from in the short term as well in perpetuity.

If you and your team are approached by a producer, be sure to consult with an entertainment lawyer, preferably one that has experience with media contracts. Review the contract and understand what its clauses and conditions mean before signing.

Chapter 8
THEORIES

For as long as humankind has puzzled over its encounters with ghosts and apparitions of the living, it has taken the next logical step of creating reasons to explain these experiences: from inhuman, godlike creatures to a recorded imprint in stone and from time slips to telepathy. Using what they think they know of the constructs of the physical world as a basis, everyone who has publicly wondered about the mechanics behind the creation and formation of ghosts has contributed to theory.

Theory is malleable and is always ripe for agreement, change, or outright rejection. Advancements in anything humankind has created began as an idea and developed into theory, which was then acted upon, experimented with, and tested before coming to a satisfying conclusion. In short, where would we be without theory?

The same holds true for delving into ghost phenomena; the early investigators were tasked with answering to a curious public and sometimes had to come up with explanations on the spot for inquiring news reporters. Variations of a theory such as "Children perceive ghosts more than adults because they're too young to know any better" seemed sensible enough to print in newspapers, were reprinted in multiple books, and became accepted as unquestionable truth in the minds of subsequent ghost researchers.

We are living in an exciting time in terms of modern, scientific equipment available to us as field researchers. If more teams would be willing to test old theory (i.e., to observe for themselves if it makes sense or not) and devise new theory to test and share, this area of study would advance exponentially.

In this chapter, we offer some of our own theories, addressing a number of aspects of ghost phenomena that many students of the paranormal will appreciate. We'll always welcome constructive discussion in our quest to advance humankind's most enduring questions.

Theory and Experimentation

In 2006 the world of paranormal interest in ghost phenomena was quietly introduced to a groundbreaking new theory posed by Richard at the back of his second publication, *Journeys into the Unknown* (Dundurn Press). This idea, dubbed the Memory Bubble (a.k.a. the Memory Matrix), was the first working theory within the context of our chosen field to see the light of day since the likes of Harry Price and members of the Society of Psychical Research posed theirs in public almost a century earlier.

For reasons unknown, though the Memory Bubble theory has been shared and discussed in hundreds of television, radio, and internet-based interviews, most paranormal-obsessed fans and investigation teams have never heard of it, much less engaged in a debate regarding its merits.

With this in mind, it is only fitting that we begin the deeper dive into our collective studies by considering Richard's original theory, which has since been expanded upon to make better sense of other ghost phenomena (such as phantoms of nonliving objects) over the ensuing years. This and other theories are shared here in the earnest hope that someone somewhere will be inspired to challenge them, expand upon them, and perhaps even design field experiments in order to test them.

The Memory Bubble/Memory Matrix Theory

The Memory Matrix is a working theory on where ghosts exist, how they build their own version of reality, and how they might interact with the living.

According to the Memory Matrix theory, a person at the end of their life will create a very real and complex reality in which they will continue to exist. This reality would include the places they lived just as they were when they were alive and would also include all the people they were used to seeing on a daily basis. Whether living or dead, it wouldn't matter, as the spirit's own mind would create from memory very real interactions and scenarios, giving the spirit the impression that they were very much alive and existing in the physical. Where it becomes confusing for these spirits is when they start to perceive the living as part of their memory matrix. It scares the living and startles the spirit.

The majority of these spirits who exist within the memory matrix are well adjusted and content; most don't even know they are dead. It is the other, smaller percentage of spirits who create hauntings, who have broken from the memory matrix and try to exist in our reality, causing problems for the living. These spirits normally carry a heavy obsession regarding a major situation from their lifetime or even a traumatic, unjust end. They usually feel they are a victim of some sort, and this obsessive behavior keeps them very close to our reality.

The fabric, their reality of space/time that formulates a memory bubble, is a frequency resonating at a specific harmonic value. The bubble contains a slice of time, devised and perceived by the entity as reality. The time it represents is out of synch with time that the living perceive. The phrase *my life flashed before my eyes* is an appropriate statement within this context. At the point of death, an individual's life will, out of memory, replay itself to the individual. The deceased will eventually select a point in time from their memory that will have deep, personal meaning to them and exist within it. It may range from an extremely happy time to something they are obsessed over, perhaps dwelling on something they did or that was done to them.

Memory Bubble Development

We never wanted to fall into a discussion of religion because we understand that this can be an extremely delicate subject. Everyone has, or should have, the freedom to follow and practice the religion of their choice. Regardless of which religion, all have the same principal messages for all of us: Be good to one another, take care of those around you, and believe in and worship a higher power.

Having said that, we must tread into the deeper water of what most religions consider a day of Judgment, or Judgment Day. There are commonalities regarding this time in Judeo–Christian and Islamic teachings, and all agree that there will be such a day. If this holds true, then the souls of people must reside somewhere prior to that day, and if not true, the soul still requires a place to be.

The memory bubble is developed out of an individual's memory, which consists of events, emotions, and experiences. People are, believe it or not, their own harshest critics, and they will, without knowing, put themselves where they need to be. People are creatures of habit and through that habit will take all of life's personal events, emotions, and experiences with them in death, involuntarily becoming what they have always been in life. They will unknowingly choose an interim place of existence.

Heaven

A peaceful afterlife, referred to as heaven in some religions, is where an individual goes when they have died, accepted and acknowledged their wrongdoings while alive, and found an enjoyable place in time where they were most happy in life. The memory bubble is then formed around that time, transferring them to an existence of peaceful harmony. These entities are quiet and exist at a vibrational frequency that members of the living will be least likely to perceive.

Hell

Hell is where individuals go when they have died but are obsessed over things they have done or that were done to them, possibly over money, property, a relationship, or other unforgivable wrongdoings. In this existence, desperate for justice, to complete an important task, right a wrong, or simply hide a crime, they straddle living reality and that of the afterlife, vibrating at a frequency the living *can* perceive, generating an eternal hell for themselves. The memory bubble they create contains all the perceived sins and fears that haunted them in life. These entities are restless and active; some may be benevolent, but many are malevolent.

Interestingly, in 1999, Pope John Paul II courted controversy when he openly mused on the nature of heaven and hell—as not real places but rather as states of mind—before audiences at the Vatican.

Heaven, *Washington Post* reporter Hanna Rosin said in late July of that same year, "is neither an abstraction *nor a physical place* in the clouds but a living and personal relationship with the Holy Trinity."

Better to think of hell, she explained the next week, as *more than a physical place,* as "the state of those who freely and definitely separate themselves from God, the source of all life and joy."[16]

Near-Death Experiences and the Memory Bubble

It has been discovered that in near-death experiences there are constant common events that occur and are reported. The first is a noise like a buzzing sound, which could be the change in frequency from this reality to the next. All report that they lose track of time; time has little meaning to them. They then enter a life review. This review normally follows a chronology, from birth to the point of death. It is at this point in the near-death experience that these people are turned back and return to their physical bodies. Had they not been resuscitated, I believe the individual would have chosen a slice of time from their life review and that time frame would have then become their new reality. Their reality contains all the things that one would find in this reality, such as sight, sound, furniture, and people living and deceased, which are created as a reasonable facsimile from the personal memory of them, and because their mental attributes are intact, they also retain modesty. This is why naked ghosts are rarely seen.

This new reality may not be exactly as it was when they were living but rather as they perceived it to be in their lifetime experience. The entire bubble resonates at a frequency beyond our perception; however, we are surrounded by these bubbles everywhere we go. Most are silent and exist in harmony, never to be known by us, but there are rare situations when these bubbles make themselves known to us in various ways. There are two specific triggers that allow this to happen.

....
16. Rosin, "Pope's Vision of Heave, Hell Riles Evangelicals"; italics added.

The first is when a spirit focuses on an important event or problem in their past life. This intense focus, not unlike a daydream, raises the spirit's emotional energy level and therefore raises the amplitude of the frequency, which allows paranormal sights, sounds, and smells to manifest in our reality. The second trigger is a highly emotionally charged memory, which causes deep thought, turmoil, and disturbance to the spirit. Roving smells are one phenomenon that may transcend the boundaries of both realities. Another is the sound of moving furniture and things breaking when there is no evidence to suggest anything has been broken or moved. These audio anomalies are simply projections created by the spirit(s) that resonate in our reality and can be perceived. Major disturbances come when the spirit perceives either a chance to communicate with the living, an opportunity to manipulate your choices and actions to produce a result they wish to see, or a threat by you to them in changing something they do not want changed or learning something they do not want you to know about their past.

Some examples include:

Case One: Private Residence (Toronto, ON)

Jeff and Jim purchased their dream home close to the beaches in an affluent community. From the beginning, the house produced strange sounds and smells, and over time, more disturbing and frightening phenomena started to emerge such as doors slamming, shadows, disembodied whispers, and missing items. A long-term investigation revealed that a man who had lived in the house and died in the home in 1958 had been recognized as a pillar of the community, holding a fairly high position within the local church. The working hypothesis was that this spirit, being from a different time and given his position in the church, fueled his prejudices against the couple now living presumptuously under his roof and was trying to get them out. The findings were presented to the couple, and within a few months they decided to sell and move away. A follow-up, informal inquiry between the investigator and the new owners found that no reported paranormal activity had been witnessed in the residence by them or their two children.

Case Two: Cawthra House (Mississauga, ON)

This historical mansion in Mississauga, Ontario, was involved in extensive renovations. The engineer had to add ductwork for the new HVAC systems, and the consensus was that the best way to do this was to lay out the systems on the existing floor and then build a new raised floor above them, concealing the work. The mansion had very high ceilings, so the addition of ten inches to the floor would hardly be noticed. The work was completed; however, some adjustments and additions had to be made. While a technician was adding a piece to the ductwork through a hatch in the newly added floor, he first heard walking coming toward him, then noticed what he would later describe as 1910s women's boots stop next to where he was working. The person wearing the boots was not standing on the recently added floor but rather on the old floor, their legs passing through the new floor. This startled the technician and caused him to jump up, injuring himself.

Sounds, such as walking on hardwood floors that are now carpeted, or sightings of figures passing through solid walls where doors once existed, suggest past events being manifested by ghosts simply recalling their former routines. This phenomena is not uncommon and has been extensively reported worldwide.

Case Three: Private Residence (Etobicoke, ON)

One evening, at the house mentioned in the book *Overshadows*, Richard and his wife arrived to visit the family who were the subjects of the haunting when a strange event occurred. Over the course of the visit, the daughter of the family suggested everyone play Ping-Pong. Everyone agreed, feeling that a little bit of fun would be a good stress relief from the events normally occurring in the house. During the game, a wild return sent the ball off the table and it struck something in open space—something they couldn't see. The ball ricocheted back and forth within a very tight, contained field between five and seven inches wide. After bouncing about ten to twelve times in rapid succession in a downward pattern, the ball fell to the floor. It was witnessed by all present.

Case Four: Harding Estate (Mississauga, ON)

During a three-year investigation at the Harding Estate, Richard recorded a female spirit there, many times, named "Anna Rita." In life, Anna Rita was a servant of the old place, and she had died long ago; however, it was noted that she still served there, meticulously cleaning the servant stairwell, which was a spectacle as it gleamed in a place otherwise beset with dust, dirt, webs, and dead spiders, and which had been boarded up for more than ten years.

Case Five: Country Heritage Park (Milton, ON)

At times, in every person's life, emotions can be so intense they may become uncontrollable. The Searcher Group believes that the trigger of a physical manifestation is the involuntary production of a negative or positive emotion. These emotions have a strong link to, but are not limited to, the individual's memory. As the individual lives within their own memory, there will be emotionally charged events that come to the surface. Thoughts, memories, or observed occurrences can easily create a dynamic response or reaction, even on a subconscious level. How we deal with emotion in life is no different in the afterlife: Feelings are formed by experience, opinions, and attitudes. The reaction to them may be extremely powerful, can be involuntary, and may even create behavior that is questionable and bizarre.

One event demonstrating a positive emotion as a trigger was observed when children on a school trip visited a house from the 1840s that was set up as a museum to show what life was like in that era. The original owner (deceased) had lost a grandchild in 1870. As the school children entered the house, the entity saw a child who closely resembled her grandson. The resulting emotion triggered a physical manifestation, and the woman appeared as a ghostly figure to the children. The feeling was not reciprocated, and the children fled the house, screaming. This situation repeated several times over the years until a medium made contact and explained to the entity that her grandson was not coming back. These incidents have not been reported to have occurred since.

Case Six: Private Residence (Etobicoke, ON)
Richard visited a family that he was working with to investigate their haunting. It was just prior to Christmas, and they were sitting in the kitchen adjacent to the living room, where a mixed tape of Christmas music was playing. An old version of "Ave Maria" began, and a girl's voice began to sing along from the living room. There was no one in the living room, and there certainly wasn't a child in the house at the time. Richard believes the time of year and the memory and emotion the song held for this spirit inspired the child to manifest audibly.

Case Seven: Private Residence (ON, Canada)

In an investigation of a teenage girl who had died by suicide, Richard was able to gain the information that she loved horses and would spend time learning about them and riding them but also hours sketching them. She may have not known that where this incident took place was at one time a large horse ranch. Richard used all this information to open a conversation about horses and the history of the property. Two manifestations occurred, however briefly. The first was the smell of a horse and leather, and the second was the slight sound of running hooves on the ground just outside the room where the test was being conducted. Another incident occurred months later when two mounted police officers patrolled through the grounds and passed the house. There came a flurry of sounds from the upstairs room and hallway, as if someone was in a rush to get down the hall to the back bedroom window to gain a glimpse of the horses.

Memory Bubble Intrusion and Clusters

In 1901 there was a case involving two English women: Anne Moberly and Eleanor Jourdain. On a trip to Paris, the two reported that while touring the grounds of Versailles, they seemed to walk into the past.[17] They saw people in period dress from the late eighteenth century, around the time of Marie Antoinette (1755–1793), and reported that the environment around them had changed, feeling heavy, depressed, and very unpleasant. This incident has been considered a time slip, where Moberly and Jourdain came into contact with a collective memory bubble, or what is termed a *cluster*.

....
17. Moberly and Jourdain, *An Adventure.*

Clusters

When spirits share specific memories of an event, the memories converge, creating what we call clusters. These combined memories can cause temporal distortions, which are referred to as time slips. People who have experienced time slips report having traveled through time to another era. The modification and expansion of a memory bubble occurs when more than one spirit in close proximity shares a specific time frame. An example would be when many people died in a single event, such as a battle or plane crash. They rely on each other's memory of that time and adapt the information to the bubble, causing the bubble to expand.

This time slip phenomenon has been reported at locations of great loss during the American Civil War, in particular Gettysburg, Pennsylvania, and Perryville, Kentucky.

The heavy, unpleasant feelings that witnesses report is due to being drawn into these events where the frequencies have a deep negative effect on our bodies; we are not meant to exist within these frequencies.

It's within this bubble that a spirit's thought process, if traumatic and powerful, may manifest into our reality, and should it be reinforced with that of other spirits, it could take on a life of its own. A manifestation could then separate from the memory bubble. This would explain the sightings of ghostly ships and trains, some of which suffered devastating fates in history. That manifestation bubble, which has detached and is not supported, seems real but quickly dissipates without warning and vanishes from the witness's view.

Scientific Exploration

Electromagnetic energy exists within each of us. Science is now examining this energy at the cellular level, leading to the belief that it is a platform for information transfer and communication from one cell to another.[18] There is also ongoing research that is now trying to redefine what death is, as it has been discovered that at the time of brain death, there remains communication at the cellular level within the body. Near-death researchers have looked at this with great interest, as subjects have reported actions and conversations within hospital emergency and operating rooms when they had already been pronounced brain-dead, only to be resuscitated. Researchers now feel the information within the body was retained by this energy at the cellular level. Once the individual was revived, they had full knowledge of what was going on while they were dead.[19] This is very exciting on its own, but if we throw into the equation the fact that energy cannot be destroyed, could this information involving an individual remain if they were not revived and their body was pronounced permanently deceased?

In 1939 Semyon Kirlian (1898–1978) discovered, by accident, what would eventually be termed the *Kirlian effect*, a photographic procedure that appears to capture the life force that surrounds every living thing.[20] It was further noted in Kirlian investigations that changes in moisture could indicate emotional changes, which affect the coronal discharges around the subject. If these photos truly demonstrate life force, then there would seem to be integrity within what I have termed the Memory Matrix. This was demonstrated with the famous photo of the leaf, which shows a leaf with the top portion cut off and removed. Amazingly, the Kirlian photo shows the aura of the entire leaf. This seems to demonstrate that even though the leaf is damaged and incomplete, there is something that *remembers* the shape integrity of the entire leaf, as displayed by the photo.

. . . .

18. Absi, "Is the Brain the Only Place That Stores Our Memories?"
19. Greyson, "Near-Death Experiences and Systems Theories."
20. Kraig, "Term: Kirlian Photography."

In 1985, at the Academy of Sciences in Moscow, a scientist was mapping a DNA sample with a laser.[21] He had fired the laser into the target chamber but had forgotten to place his specimen slide into the target area. What occurred was an image of the previous DNA sample, as though it was still present within the chamber even though it had been removed. The equipment was inspected and further tests were conducted. They all produced the same result. It seemed the laser was being influenced by what is now termed the *DNA phantom effect*. It was determined that when the sample was removed, something remained, invisible to the human eye, which could influence light waves and leave an imprint.[22] Could the energy signature of DNA leave a signature standing wave in its environment? Could these invisible lines of force be part of the integrity of the Memory Matrix?

In quantum physics, *quantum coherence* means that subatomic particles are able to cooperate with one another. Coherence establishes communication. Particles seem to be aware of each other and are interconnected by bands of electromagnetic fields. Let's imagine for a moment that they operate like a tuning fork, and as information cascades along these lines of electromagnetic fields, they all begin to resonate together. It is when this occurs and they move into a phase synch that they all begin acting like one giant wave. It then becomes difficult to tell them apart. If some action is done to one of them, it will affect them all.

It was discovered in 1923, by a Russian medical professor, Alexander G. Gurvich (1874–1954), that DNA is an essential source of light energy in the form of biophotons, or what he termed

----

21. Eells, "Cleve Backster."
22. Braden, *The Divine Matrix*.

mitogenetic rays.[23] These rays exist in every living organism and operate into the ultraviolet spectrum of light. This may also be what produces the aura seen by the Kirlian effect. In this respect, DNA could then, in essence, be the master tuning fork, playing at a particular frequency, which would start a cascade of information that all other particles would fall in line and follow.[24]

Ions are charged atoms; they can be negative (more electrons) or positive (more protons). A negative charge and a positive charge will attract each other, where two negatives or two positives will repel each other. Charged objects will create an electric field around themselves. Ions that become trapped will stay together and may produce a densely packed cloud. The ions within the cloud move by repelling and attracting each other. Ions can be generated in abundance whenever energy is transferred into the air. One method of transference is ultraviolet light. Another is positive ions, which can cause a heavy, oppressed feeling.

Ions and static electricity have produced results that can be studied in a lab and reproduced. Results include hair standing on end, goose flesh, cold spots, and sensations of being touched. Further, there can be various visual phenomena, such as glowing balls of light. Static discharge can produce snapping, crackling, and banging noises as well as water in the form of condensation. All these phenomena have been reported in haunted locations.

What if something of us does survive after death, something that retains intelligence, emotion, and memory? What would it look like? Could it have some of the characteristics found in the examples above and exist as a small ball of invisibility just beyond our

....

23. "Gurwitsch (Gurvich), Alexander Gavrilovich."
24. Volodyaev and Beloussov. "Revisiting the Mitogenetic Effect of Ultra-Weak Photon Emission."

perception? Could this be what Dr. Duncan MacDougall (1866–1920) of Haverhill, Massachusetts, observed and reported in his experiments?[25] He reported in his death observation experiments, shared in *American Medicine* in April of 1907, an unexplained loss of weight of between 1½ to 2½ ounces from his subjects at the time of death.[26] Could this be something of the soul?

Perceiving Ghosts: The Eyes and Ears Have It

A ghost's existence seems to involve several stages. They are invisible beyond our perception or stringy shadows, and some are a form of apparition. Let's start with the shadows and how and why we might see them. As Richard combed through hundreds of reports and articles, there seemed to be patterns and consistencies that emerged. First, Richard had to understand how the human eye works, which led him to a multitude of medical texts and several doctors and optometrists.

Every person has two types of vision. Foveal, which is direct or focused vision, is our primary vision, as it is perfect for seeing details. The other is peripheral vision, which is suited for detecting and seeing shadows. Peripheral vision isn't used often, as we are no longer predators hunting for our food and on guard against attacks from other predators. Our peripheral is designed to allow low-resolution vision: motion detection at 180 degrees at a wide range of illuminations. Foveal vision uses cones (color vision), which have filters that prevent a large portion of ultraviolet light from reaching the retina. Peripheral uses rods (black-and-white vision), which are sensitive to ultraviolet light. In a majority of people, the UV filters do

....

25. Ishida, "Rebuttal to Claimed Refutations of Duncan MacDougall's Experiment."
26. MacDougall, "Hypothesis Concerning Soul Substance."

not completely filter out all of the UV light, as there are small gaps at the corners of their eyes (peripheral). The phenomenon is generally experienced inside a building. Further, an article appeared in the *Journal of the Society of Psychical Research* in 1998 that reported several instances of sensing and sightings of ghostly phenomena. All visual input related to the phenomena was always detected by the peripheral vision.[27]

This information is significantly important, and we believe the structure and development of the eye has a great deal to do with seeing ghosts. Spirit composition reflects UV light at certain points of the manifestation process: it is within the UV-A spectrum of 380 to 315 nanometers. It is the UV-A light that is the basis of the research, as UV-A is found both indoors and outdoors, where UV-B 314 to 280 nanometers and UV-C 279 to 200 nanometers is not found indoors.

> *Human eyesight:* A majority of people will visually respond to wavelengths from about 380 to 750 nanometers or, in terms of frequency, 400 to 790 terahertz. There is a great deal of the electromagnetic spectrum humans cannot see unaided. The UV filters within the human eye develop over time, and with age, the lens of the eye hardens and becomes yellow, thus decreasing the eye's absorbing ability, blocking out more UV radiation. UV will enter the eyes of children and infants at full strength, which could be why children perceive more phenomena than adults.
>
> *Animal eyesight:* Animals often respond to things we cannot easily detect, and both dogs and cats have extremely

. . . .
27. Tandy, "The Ghost in the Machine."

good vision in the dark, allowing them to detect movement in low lighting. They can also see within the ultraviolet spectrum of light, as they rarely develop the ability to block out UV light due to their short life spans.

Light and Shadows: How Most Adults Perceive Visual Ghost Phenomena

There are numerous reports of people relating the same phenomena, which are now being termed *shadow people*. (See "Shadow People" in chapter 1.) This phenomenon is not new. People have long been seeing black or dark image movement out of their peripheral vision, only to have it disappear when they turn their heads. Is it possible that these shadow people exist in the UV spectrum of light? Or, in better terms, do they reflect UV light waves? When the observer turns to look directly at the image, does the UV filter within the eye instantly block it from perception, vanishing the image? (This may be why monks in medieval times placed small mirrors beside their noses. The mirrors would have allowed them to see roaming spirits in their peripheral vision.)

Richard began studying several photos of apparitions reflected in mirrors. The photos didn't show an apparition in the room, per se, but clearly showed an image *within* the mirror. (See "Mirrors" in chapter 1.) The camera flash, when fired, not only flared visible light but UV light. It was the UV flare that, when impacting and interacting with a spirit's energy signature passing through this field, left a split-second imprint upon the mirror or reflective surface and, acting like the emulsions of film, lasted long enough for the camera to capture the image. This produced a photo image not of the spirit but of a reflection of the spirit. After discussing much of my theory on UV waves and their relationship with spirit energy with my associate, John Mullan, he summed it up with an analogy:

It is like dust particles floating around the room; you can't see them, but regardless they are still there. It's when you catch a sun beam shining in through a window the floating dust is suddenly illuminated.[28]

There seems to be something solid to the makeup of a spirit. Normally, when a person passes close by our surveillance cameras, the lens iris quickly adjusts according to the change in lighting conditions; however, this action has also been noted many times when *no one* (living) has been present, let alone passing the camera. The iris has inexplicably adjusted itself, making the background lighting appear to darken and then brighten. Interestingly, while the camera has made these adjustments, clear, disembodied footfalls have simultaneously been captured by the camera microphone at times, suggesting something unseen was indeed present. We suspect an entity inhabited the UV spectrum portion of light the camera lens is sensitive to, hence the triggered iris adjustment.

Hearing

Hearing is a complex mechanism. Within the ear is the organ of Corti, which contains thousands of hair cells. When a wave or burst of energy passes over these hairs, it causes them to move, sending impulses to the cochlear nerve and then on to the cerebral cortex. The brain then interprets the information received. Could a silent burst of energy bypass the outer ear and cause the organ of Corti to detect and transfer information to the brain? It would depend greatly upon how agitated the environment became. Subtle messages would require electronic assistance, such as what is found in a cassette tape recorder.

....
28. Personal communication with author, 2002.

The pre-emphasis chip captures sound outside the normal hearing range and boosts its signal into the audible range.

> *Human hearing:* Humans can detect sounds in a frequency range from about 20 Hz to 20 kilohertz (kHz). Human infants can hear frequencies slightly higher than 20 kHz. As we mature we often lose higher frequency ranges, to about 15 to 17 kHz.
>
> *Dog hearing:* Typically, a dog's range of hearing is approximately 40 Hz to 60 kHz.
>
> *Cat hearing:* Typically, a cat's range of hearing is approximately 48 Hz to 85 kHz.

Case Study: Sound Manipulation

Another interesting observation was made on several occasions of what Richard calls *insertion*, which is similar to telepathy. It is where the spirit can project a sound or a voice directly toward a specific person or group of people. This can also occur with a group of people within a location simultaneously, with each reporting the content of the message to be different. However, the content that was heard caused each person to react as if another person had initiated the action, requiring a response.

For example, at one point during the *Overshadows* investigation, Kellie was upstairs and Shelby was downstairs; both heard the other call them. They responded and met at the stairs, asking what the other had wanted. Neither had called out to the other.

Another example took place the night Jon, Al, and Richard were conducting an investigation in the vacant house next door to Al's. They were in the middle of an intense line of questioning when their attention was diverted by the sound of the back door slamming shut. Their response was immediate, but they found no one there. The videotape on their fixed camera clearly shows them moving in response to the sound we all heard, yet the sound of the door itself was not captured on the portable audio recorder. When they took a break, they left both audio and video systems set to record in the same location they had been in when the incident occurred. The tapes recorded the team leaving and the sound of the door closing.

Electromagnetic Energy and Emotion

As investigators we hear reports of situations within haunted locations from people who experience emotions that are not their own but rather shared with them or forced upon them by an unknown source.

Richard wishes to explore the correlation between weak electromagnetic fields. It is a difficult journey because science understands that scientific teams, given the exact same information, may come to very different conclusions, and to add further complication, scientific teams may also arrive at the same conclusion by using very different methods.

First, we have to understand what brain waves are. They are the result of neural activity within the brain, which creates its own electromagnetic spectrum measured in hertz. Brain waves are classified as delta (0.1 to 4 Hz), theta (4 to 8 Hz), alpha (8 to 12 Hz), beta (12 to 30 Hz), and gamma (30 Hz and above).

Influence from EMF

It has been noted that depending on the intensity, externally produced EMF can create disorders in the brain's neurotransmitters, causing abnormal emotional behavior. Further scientific study has shown that electromagnetic waves affect emotions as well as our bodies directly by altering brain function and nerve impulses.

Therapeutic frequency tests have shown that using specific tones to alter brain waves usually target the alpha brain wave, between 8 and 12 Hz; this therapy heightens imagination, visual memory, learning, and concentration and is the gateway to the subconscious mind and the voice of your intuition.

Theta brain waves range from 4 to 7.5 Hz and are linked to emotions, the subconscious mind, and REM sleep. A majority of adults only experience theta when asleep, but theta has been noted as dominant in children, even when awake. Children show significantly higher theta activity. Theta enhances the ability to process emotions, connects to our intuition, and provides subconscious processing. This difference could possibly explain why children may report more paranormal experiences.

The theta brain wave range is tied to experiencing very strong emotions. Is it possible that emotion could be transferred using a medium of EMF?

In cases where no electromagnetic anomalies are discovered within a highly controlled haunted location, we suggest that when subjects display and report feeling emotions that are not their own, samples of EMF should be taken immediately. Should the investigator have a frequency counter, then they should search for stray frequencies. In many cases, Richard has discovered a frequency of 4 Hz present without any source or explanation in the vicinity. A great deal of further research is required for this theory, but it could lead to other technological methods of communication with the dead.

Cultural and Religious Beliefs

Whether you travel to conduct paranormal research or investigate locally, it is important in a multicultural world to have some knowledge of different belief systems. It allows you to understand the client's mindset when they report activity, and it may explain why so many people automatically assume what they are dealing with is either evil or demonic.

Judaism: Within Judaism, there is the belief in possessive souls of the dead. One is sinister, known as the dybbuk, and the other is known as ibbur, which can haunt a location but is believed to be more of a positive entity that can bring messages or prophecies to the living.

Christianity: To members of the Christian faith, ghosts are actually demons in disguise. There are a few denominations that believe some ghosts are tied to the earthly plane in order to fulfill unfinished business or to seek repentance.

Islam: Within this religion there is the belief that when a person dies the soul leaves the body and is gone forever. However, there is also a belief in jinn and devils, the enemies of humankind that walk the earth behaving mischievously, causing problems for the living and leading people down the path of sin.

North American Indigenous cultures: These beliefs vary greatly, and it's important to not generalize when investigating. Some believe that ghosts can have a negative influence on the living and that apparitions can haunt the living, while others have no fear of ghosts and believe that they are harmless. They may even seek out ghosts to ask for their protection.

Mexican: Here, life and death are intertwined, where death is just a continuation of life. Life is a dream world, and only in death is one truly awake. Every November the Day of the

Dead is celebrated. It is during this time that departed souls may visit the world of the living.

Asian: In Asian cultures, the spirits of the dead are revered and shown great respect. Precautions are taken to never offend them to avoid wrathful consequences.

Buddhism: Most Buddhists accept that ghosts exist within a plane that overshadows our world. Buddhists believe that hungry ghosts must be cared for by the community and celebrate the Yu Lan Pen, a time when people worship and show great respect toward the dead.

Chinese: In China, the celebration of several ghost festivals are observed, including the Hungry Ghost Festival. During this festival, which takes places in the seventh lunar month and lasts fourteen days, it is believed that the gates of hell are opened to release hungry ghosts to wander the earth in search of food and take revenge upon those who wronged them in life.

Taoism: Taoists celebrate the Zhongyuan Festival, honoring the memories of their forefathers.

Indian: Ghosts and a whole host of other supernatural creatures are revered across India. A *bhoot* is the spirit of a deceased person. The belief in demons is widespread, and they are believed to be harmful to humans. There are many practices and rituals to counter the destructive forces these entities possess.

African: It is believed that the forefathers remain and inhabit the community as spirits, and that in death a spirit maintains their knowledge and identity. Known as *bazimu*, they return to the places that they knew in life and once inhabited.

A majority of people believe bazimu are malevolent, and many rituals and practices must be followed so as to not provoke these spirits. Failure to follow these rituals may cause one to be haunted. A spirit can transform into a demon (*jachien*) if that person had died a dishonorable death or by suicide.

Japanese: Traditional beliefs hold that all people have a spirit (*reikon*). At the time of death, the spirit enters a purgatory until all funeral rites have been completed, allowing the spirit to join their ancestors. Those spirits that are not at rest become ghosts (*yūrei*). There are also beliefs in demons. The *oni* is a very powerful evil spirit and a *tengu* can possess humans.

The Stone Tape Theory Debunked: Synchronicity Within a Haunting

In some cases, a haunting can involve synchronicity. In other words, a spirit may reenact particular moments from their former physical lifetime that are perceived (sometimes briefly) during ours.

Regarding the Stone Tape theory, researchers incorrectly catalogued instances of spirit synchronicity as mindless, unalterable recordings of events that appeared to replay themselves action-for-action indefinitely. It was speculated that these patterns of activity were phantom holograms that could not be changed or influenced by the living and that they were imprinted on certain environs utilizing materials used in the manufacture of analog tape media.

The Searcher Group commends anyone with the confidence and wherewithal to put forward theories in this field. Doing so promotes discussion and provokes further testing; there would be no advancements in *any* field of study without imagination and original theory. Unfortunately, as enterprising as the Stone Tape theory was, subsequent study has belied its worth as a viable one.

Not every manifestation of a repeated pattern or "place memory" incident occurs within one kind of environment. Not every site includes the required elements (such as quartz crystals) that the Stone Tape theory hinges on, nor do these locations require certain witnesses with special brain waves or psychic abilities to perceive the repeated phenomena. This is illustrated by video cameras' ability to accomplish this, too.

No, these are simply cases of synchronicity between spirits. Their reenacted and manifested memories are briefly perceived by the living (sometimes captured by modern recording technology) and reported over the course of several years. The following sections share ideas that may explain why these manifestations occur, and there is also theory on how one may effectively interrupt and stop the cycle altogether.

Theory 1

The spirit could have been involved with a tragic and traumatic end and doesn't like or understand their end-of-life situation. While working through this problem, their memories and emotions are fueled by their energy and the spirit replays occurrences familiar to them. These collide or intersect with our reality, becoming what is traditionally defined as a haunting. Oftentimes, these projected replay hauntings occur apart from the presence of the living witnesses. In other words, they are not inspired to be "activated" or performed in response to the actions of a living person.

Theory 1A

Any actions by you or others within the location could be seen or appear similar and therefore re-enforce the spirit's current reality, making you part of that reality. This could be good or bad depending how you and others are perceived, either friend or foe, and the spirit's actions and reactions toward you will be—in their eyes—appropriate. You could be Ed from 2022, but they may see you as Uncle Joe from 1935.

Theory 2

When it comes to the layout of furniture, homes can be funny. Some rooms, depending on the location of windows, doors, and closets, may be limited in the ways they can be set up. For some spirits, the furniture layout could be exactly as it was during their living time in the dwelling and might be so familiar that it re-enforces their reality.

In some reported hauntings, people recount seeing figures standing around their bed and looking down at them. It is very possible the spirits are not seeing that living person at all but a friend or loved one who was sick or dying in that exact same spot many years ago.

There are two things an investigator can do to try to change the scenario.

First, they can research as much about the property and the people who once lived there as possible, looking for that important piece of historical information that can be used to either change the spirit's view of the event or clarify what happened. Doing so may end the cycle for them. This, of course, is extremely difficult, as a great deal of historical data may not be available.

The second (and potentially easier) option is to alter the layout of the room where the incident is occurring. Doing so could interrupt the spirit memory process.

Time, in most cases, can be irrelevant, as the concept of time rarely means anything to spirits, and their sense of time is completely out of synch with ours. Paul once recorded an EVP of a mother trying to feed her children lunch—at ten at night.

In one such case, a client called Richard saying their child was being woken up around two in the morning. Richard advised them to change the location of the child's bed, and the disturbances ceased.

The Stone Tape or Recurring Residual Haunting Paradox

We, as researchers, either hear of or read about recurring hauntings where a manifestation appears in the same place at the same time on very specific dates, sometimes anniversaries or even weekly depending on the story. They have been quite conveniently termed *residual hauntings*, and yet, as investigators, we can't produce any evidence of their existence simply because when we show up, the cycle is broken and nothing occurs. Is this because our presence changes the dynamics of the ghostly event? If so, might that signify intelligence?

Poltergeists

There is a theory that poltergeist activity is due to an unknown supernatural force that may be connected to a living person. The person they are connected to may be either male or female but are predominantly female. The theory further suggests that the person will normally be an adolescent coming into puberty. The poltergeist activity can be caused by emotional stress or trauma that may cause spontaneous recurring psychokinesis and unconsciously affect the environment.

One of the problems with this theory is that vacant locations have demonstrated such activity, as well as inhabited locations where no children are present.

What about other hauntings where a wide assortment of activity is experienced? Does it make sense that a spirit can only go so far, so when things get tough, they have to call in their poltergeist friend to cause physical damage?

There are hundreds of theories. The idea is to find ones that interest you and study them, take them into the field and test them, and see if they apply to what your experience tells you. Build experiments and record the data. This is the only way to make progress. If every old theory were correct, the question of life after death would no longer be a mystery.

Project Switch

Here is an experiment Richard designed in the 1990s. This isn't an easy experiment to conduct, as there is a lot of work involved. You have probably seen a fouled-up version of this on TV, as paranormal entertainers have no time or interest in doing the hard work and instead demand instantaneous results. Thus, provocation was born.

Unfortunately, we cannot bring these theories and projects into a lab to test and study; it's all a matter of fieldwork. However, once a location is established, to conduct a test the area can and must be stringently controlled.

An investigator must conduct a great deal of study on each individual case. The identity of the spirit, if possible, is of utmost importance. If this can be known, then the investigator should proceed with a full background check of the individual. Not every case will produce desirable results. This could be simply due to the investigator not being able to identify the subject or not being able to collect vital information on the subject.

When this information is successfully collected, the investigator can then attempt to replicate an environment that will relate specifically to the spirit being investigated. It is at this point that the investigator must build a psychological scenario to engage the subject. Having done this, it should trigger a memory response from the spirit person, which should cause some type of manifestation to occur. These events can then be recorded and analyzed under scientific conditions.

Remember that there are many variables to consider, and it may take more than one experiment.

The psychological motivation and involvement with a spirit for this type of experiment is shown in the following procedure:

- The investigator must attempt to establish who is involved (deceased) along with as much of their personal history as possible.
- The investigator must collect evidence and document the events as they are played out in the haunting.
- Next comes an analysis of all data and the probable nature of what seems to be the message or problem being played out in these events.
- The investigator must then design the best scenario in which to proceed and prepare a psychological event that will deeply involve the spirit with particular attention to the displayed events (i.e., what seems to be important to the spirit).
- The next step is to control the location. Seal the area to keep unwanted noise out, and safeguard against unauthorized persons.
- The investigator should then shut off all unneeded electrical equipment and set up monitoring equipment within the target area. This equipment should ideally be controlled by remote means. No one, not even the investigator, should remain in the target area once the experiment commences.
- The investigator can then commence the scenario, recording all data from the target area.

Building Theory

During an investigation a few years ago, we discovered the spirit of a young boy who had died on the property. The boy had some disabilities in his lifetime and was not treated well by his parents and the neighborhood children.

However, this boy's spirit seemed to exude a special skill, which caused the team great initial concern. He could produce monsters that seemed to be present as his protectors. (Over time, we found that these phantoms posed no threat and would neither interact nor respond to us.)

To Build a Theory

To build theory, you must first define what the problem or question is. In this instance involving the boy's spirit:

1. Could a person (living or dead) conjure entities using their mind?
2. Is there anything in historical data that might account for this type of phenomenon?

Would it be possible that the spirit of a child—frightened by our presence and our investigative activity—could draw from his memory of fantastical creatures from books and stories and use his imagination (and heightened anxiety) to manifest phantom likenesses perceivable in our reality?

As investigators, we must search for all available information related to our question, from all possible sources. These sources must include, but are not limited to, the body of work available within the many branches of parapsychology and psychology, the many disciplines of science, and books, news articles, and papers on related subjects.

Thoughts Forms

A thought form is described as an entity wholly created by the mind, either unconsciously or consciously. This entity, once developed, can separate from the one who created it and build a life of its own, becoming a force in our world. The term *thought form* was introduced to Western civilization as far back as 1905 and inspired by the Tibetan tulpa, the pooka in Germanic and Celtic cultures, and the jinn in Arabic cultures.[29] Thought forms are believed to give rise to poltergeist and demonic phenomena.

During her time in the Himalayas, author Alexandra David-Néel (1868–1969) claimed that she had intentionally produced a tulpa. This thought form took on the appearance of a short, fat, jolly monk. It was at this time that other people around her began seeing this entity as well. She explained in her 1932 book, *Magic and Mystery in Tibet*, that the tulpa had developed its own will and become malevolent.

Jan Baptist van Helmont (1580–1644), a Flemish chemist, physician, and physiologist, believed that we have the ability to use our minds and the power of imagination to create real entities.

Annie Besant (1847–1933) and Charles Webster Leadbeater (1854–1934) wrote a book on the subject entitled *Thought-Forms* (1905). In it, they speculated that various emotions could combine with a deep concentration of thought to create thought forms, which could be either benevolent or malevolent and possibly become a destructive or metaphysical force.

....

29. Besant and Leadbeater, *Thought-Forms*; David-Néel, *Magic and Mystery in Tibet*; Parker and Puhle, *Thoughtforms*.

Conjuring Philip

In the 1970s, the Toronto Society for Psychical Research, under Dr. A. R. G. Owen, assembled a group of eight people chosen directly from its membership. Collectively, they wanted to try a thought form experiment and wrote a short biography of a person they named Philip Aylesford, an aristocratic Englishman living in the time of Oliver Cromwell. Once this character's backstory was created, the experimenters went to work trying to communicate with him using various methods, such as table turning, knocks, and séances, over several sessions. Incredibly, the group was very successful in bringing "Philip" to life, producing a great number of phenomena just short of a physical manifestation.[30]

The Shadow

There is a three-story house in New York City's Greenwich Village that is reportedly haunted; it was investigated by paranormal author Hans Holzer (1920–2009). The home, located at 12 Gay Street, has been the scene of many unexplained haunting phenomena going back decades, and there have been multiple reports of a particular phantom roaming the house. Several witnesses described the apparition as a man whose face was always hidden by shadow but had shining eyes. The apparition exuded youth and health and was always described as wearing evening clothes, a cape, and a hat.

Novelist Walter B. Gibson (1897–1985), the creator of Lamont Cranston (alter ego of *The Shadow* of 1930s pulp fiction fame), once lived in the house and visualized the Shadow character roaming the premises as he wrote.

. . . .
30. Owen and Sparrow, *Conjuring Up Philip.*

According to famed illustrator and writer Garth Haslam, the amount of energy Gibson would pour into his creations was astounding. He would "work on multiple stories at once on different typewriters, wandering back and forth as he had the next set of ideas for each story. He would also type until his fingers were swollen and bleeding, and produced on average from 1931 to 1949 two full *Shadow* novels a month … along with other writing projects related and not."[31]

Though Gibson wasn't a believer in ghosts, he concluded the apparition was a product of his own imagination in the form of a psychic projection, which was encountered in later years by subsequent residents.

"Poltergeist" Cases

Thought forms demonstrate a need for an extended consciousness to exist, a consciousness capable of creating entities as a result of extreme emotions and personal desires. Under these conditions, it is theorized that thought forms can develop their own sense of identity and may act and interact within our reality.

William Roll, a leading expert in poltergeists, believed thought forms (or, in his words, "extended personalities") could become a field of interacting forces and might very well develop into what is observed as a classic poltergeist perceived as an independent entity.[32]

In 2017 Adrian Cho, scientist and staff writer for *Science*, wrote an article titled "Quantum Experiment in Space Confirms that Reality Is What You Make It." In the experiment described, a photon could behave like a particle or a wave depending on how it was measured. To test the theory in terms of quantum mechanics, the science team

....
31. Haslam, "1966."
32. Roll, *The Poltergeist.*

bounced photons off satellites. The team held off on their predictions until the experiment was well past the point at which the photon would become either a wave or a particle, yet their delayed predictions were correct.[33]

Theoretically, it would seem that the spirit child our team encountered could indeed create and manifest thought forms of entities developed from his imagination and memory.

Now what we need to do as investigators is discover a means to prove it.

Is it possible that the memory of who and what we are remains in the nonphysical? Let's examine some supportive information.

Experiment 1

Quantum biologist Vladimir Poponin and colleague Peter Gariaev, conducting DNA research at the Russian Academy of Sciences, believe they have found an underlying field of energy. Their experimentation took place between 1993 and 2000 and the results have been termed the *DNA Phantom Effect*.[34]

Poponin and Gariaev were experimenting with photons and human DNA inside a vacuum. Within the experiment they found that the DNA somehow influenced the photons, shaping them into regular patterns through an invisible force. The scientists stated there was nothing in conventional physics that would allow for this. An even bigger discovery was when the DNA was removed and the experiment was run again. Poponin described the light as behaving

. . . .

33. Cho, "Quantum Experiment in Space Confirms that Reality Is What You Make It."

34. Peshawaria, "Quantum Mechanics, Spirituality and Leadership."

"surprisingly and counter-intuitively." Somehow the DNA phantom effect was still influencing the photons.[35]

Experiment 2

In the 1990s, Dr. Cleve Backster (1924–2013) was a specialist for the CIA. He designed experiments for the Army as part of an ongoing project. He had pioneered research on how human intention can affect plants, which led to the military experiments. Samples of DNA were collected from volunteers and moved to another part of the building to be studied and monitored. Each volunteer was then subjected to video images to stimulate emotional response. It was noted that when the volunteer demonstrated emotional highs and lows, their DNA responded with powerful electrical activity even though the donor and sample were in different parts of the building, separated by hundreds of feet. The observation was that they acted as if somehow still physically connected.[36]

Another experiment was carried out. This time the volunteers and their DNA samples were separated by a distance of hundreds of miles. The experimenters found the same results. The responses between the two at this distance were monitored by an atomic clock. The measurement between the emotional response of both was zero, being simultaneous.

The outcome of these experiments led scientists to believe that human emotion can physically shape our reality, and in the first experiment, the DNA that no longer existed within the tube somehow retained shape and memory integrity even though the DNA sample wasn't present.

. . . .

35. Martin, "Your DNA Communicates with Light."
36. Eells, "Cleve Backster."

The memory of what we are may be retained in the afterlife, maintaining the integrity of what we should look like. Richard calls this simply *factory settings*. We currently do not understand how this works. Possibly some clues may be found in the experiments Dr. Duncan MacDougall started with the weight of the soul, or possibly it has everything to do with quantum superposition.

Terminal Lucidity

What is termed *terminal lucidity*, or *paradoxical lucidity*, is a phenomenon that has occurred going back decades. It involves those suffering from dementia or Alzheimer's who have lost the ability to function and remember daily events and loved ones. Then, without explanation, they wake up one morning with full cognitive abilities and normal behavior. They pass away shortly afterward.

It has also been observed that people on their death beds face the same phenomenon. They experience a surge of energy, clear thinking, and alertness just prior to death. This often occurs very abruptly and can give false hope to family members.

The paranormal theory is that death can be a reset for the individual, allowing them to be completely restored as they move into the afterlife.

The Ruminating Mind

As Dr. Joseph Aaron Shrand notes in *Psychology Today*, traumatic experiences, deep emotional events, and even severe disappointment can create memories that people replay over and over in an endless loop. This can pull the person into depression and impair the ability to process emotions. The longer the person focuses on an experience, the more it will hold them to that place and moment in time.[37] Does this sound like the basis for a haunting to you?

Behind anger there is fear and disappointment. We believe the most difficult feeling for a human to tolerate is that of powerlessness.

These emotions are very powerful for both the living and the dead, and they may cement us to a particular place or frame of mind. This may happen even more so in death, as these events can become ever more consuming to the point of obsession.

In Summary

The spirit is outside of our perception, existing within its memory bubble; occasionally some action occurs that serves as a switch to synchronize the two realities, allowing them to collide in space and time. Have you ever had a dream where a sound around you in the waking world, possibly a clock radio going off, was incorporated into the dream, becoming part of it instead of waking you up? This is similar to what is taking place. This synchronicity occurs when the spirit memory perceives a living individual as part of their memory bubble, due to a resemblance or a simple convenience, causing the spirit to come forward to interact and emotions to escalate. It is at this point of interaction that the two realities merge.

The memory could seem like a routine as they work through a particular problem or event, playing it over and over. The amount of emotional energy behind these thoughts can cause the memory to be projected outward into our reality and may be witnessed by the living. These events are misidentified as residual hauntings.

. . . .
37. Shrand, "A Simple Technique to Manage Anxiety."

CONCLUSION

We and all parapsychologists await the results
of future research into this all-important area.
Scarcely any information could be as significant to the human
race as the knowledge of human existence after physical death.
–Elizabeth McAdams and Raymond Bayless,
The Case for Life After Death, 1981

This manual was created to provide educational information on a subject that has no definable answers. It proposes processes that have garnered some of the best results in investigation and research to date. It also provides ideas on new ways of thinking and suggestions to assist the investigator in how to test and build their own theory. This accumulated work will only be a success if it can motivate investigators and researchers alike to not only think about what they are doing, but also how they go about doing it; to separate fact from fiction, finding the path to enlightenment instead of TV land; and to be open-minded and establish professional relationships with like-minded people who may hold small pieces of the puzzle we are assembling. It is our sincerest hope that this manual assists you with making some of the greatest advancements in the study of life after death, ghosts, and hauntings.

—*Richard Palmisano and Peter J. Roe*

ACKNOWLEDGMENTS

It amazes and somewhat saddens me, when I sit down to consider acknowledgments, how rarely I share my feelings with those around me. I have great hope that you all know how important you are to me. To my wife, who keeps me pointed in the right direction: What would I do without you? To my brother Paul, who has stood beside me and shared so many adventures together: We dare not count them all; you made it that much more interesting—just wouldn't be the same without you. To my partner Peter Roe, who shares the same passion for solving mysteries and works (almost) as hard as I do at solving them: Thanks for being there. To all my team members past and present: Thank you for all the hard work you have done and the sacrifices you have made. To those who read my work, please be aware how I appreciate all of you for allowing me to share my thoughts and discoveries with you. No one person can know everything. Thus, it is important to establish and maintain relationships, important in life and just as important when trying to tackle such a monumental question as the existence of life after death. Life is like a puzzle, and the people around us carry small pieces to that puzzle. It isn't just those who constantly agree with everything you believe that should remain close at hand but those who sometimes disagree with your ideas or theories; it can be these opposing opinions that lead to new thoughts and new connections that lead to a great discovery. This is why I not only greatly value those I work with in my quest to understand the paranormal but also seek out those with similar interests, for within opposing ideas may emerge great discoveries.

—*Richard Palmisano*

* * *

I am nothing without the enduring love and support of family and friends; I thank you *all* for bearing with me through thick and thin. Naturally, this sentiment extends to my Searcher Group family, as I was accepted as a full-fledged member in 2010. Thank you, Richard and Paul Palmisano, for your guidance and faith. It is a genuine honor to be learning from the various firsthand frights (and wonders) you've experienced for well over four decades. It's an even greater honor to call you friends. To the shorter-term Searcher Group participants, I thank you, too; your involvement has helped shape my own growth as a team leader. Thank you to every client that entrusts us to care for and respect their properties *and* their ghosts. Thank you to every impartial historian and "heritage nut" who has aided our work. Finally, I want to express sincere gratitude to the pioneers of parapsychology studies who began the search for answers to life after life and have themselves left the physical plane. They are all familiar with the intricacies of existence on the other side of the veil by now, so how or why it is they have not made an effort to educate their equally curious descendants is perhaps the *second* greatest mystery.

The longevity of the perplexity behind ghost phenomena proves that the answers we seek are far larger and more numerous, and the questions likely unsolvable by any one explorer alone. True searchers group to combine their efforts, and all of us stand on the shoulder bones of giants.

—Peter J. Roe

GLOSSARY OF
PARANORMAL
TERMINOLOGY

afterlife: The continuance of life after physical death.

angel: Spiritual being that performs the work of God.

anomaly: Something unusual that does not conform to current scientific standard rules or laws.

apparition: The visual materialization of person or animal that is not physical.

apport: The materialization of an object, seemingly out of thin air.

asport: The disappearance or vanishing of an object without any known method.

astral body: An ethereal body or vehicle one's consciousness occupies when traveling outside their physical body. Often the astral body resembles that of the traveler in appearance.

astral plane: A spiritual world which exists beyond our physical world.

astral projection: The departure of one's consciousness from their physical body. Unlike out-of-body experiences connected to near-death situations, astral travel is often performed intentionally.

astrology: The study of the positions of celestial bodies, believing they influence natural events and human affairs.

aura: An invisible energy that surrounds all living things. See *Kirlian photography*.

automatic writing: A method used by mediums to obtain information from the spirit world. The theory is that a spirit can use the hands of a medium to transcribe information or relay a message.

Bodhi Switch (a.k.a. Awareness Switch): A theoretical mind signal that regulates one's perception of paranormal phenomena. Once activated, the percipient is instantaneously disconnected from free-flowing communication with a ghost or spirit energy, as if the realization or awareness of the "impossibility" of such contact triggers the detachment.

brain waves: Electrical impulses in the brain through which an individual's behavior, emotions, and thoughts are communicated between neurons. Brain waves occur at various frequencies and can be measured by using an electroencephalogram (EEG). They are measured in hertz (Hz), defined as one cycle per second. Brain waves are known as delta (0.1 to 4 Hz), theta (4 to 8 Hz), alpha (8 to 12 Hz), beta (12 to 30 Hz), and gamma (30 Hz and above).

case study: The investigation of a specific subject.

channeling: A method in which a spirit can communicate directly through a medium, usually while they are in a trance state.

clairaudience: The ability to detect auditory frequencies beyond normal human hearing.

clairalience: The ability to detect scents or smells outside of the normal range.

clairsentience: A general term for clairvoyance and clairaudience; it occurs in the form of extrasensory perception (ESP) through physical sensations or smells.

clairvoyance: Intuitive insight or perceptiveness about people, places, objects, or past events via extrasensory perception (ESP).

cold reading: A technique utilized by entertainers or fraudulent mediums who use open-ended questions, make general statements, and gain personal information in order to make people believe they are dealing with elements of the mystical or supernatural.

collective apparition: A rare type of sighting in which more than one person witnesses the same apparition or unexplained phenomena.

crisis apparition: A "ghost" of a person who is seriously ill, injured, or at the point of death. Not to be confused with a doppelgänger. See *doppelgänger.*

deathbed vision: Phenomena experienced by those close to the time of death; commonly visions of predeceased family members or friends and sometimes of religious figures.

déjà vu: An impression or familiarity of having seen or experienced a situation before.

demon: A nonhuman entity referred to in religious texts as evil.

demonology: The study of demons.

divination: Ability to obtain knowledge of future events by way of omens.

divining rod: A narrow, forked wooden or metal rod used by a dowser to indicate the location and presence of underground water sources, precious minerals, or sometimes oil beds. See *dowsing*.

doppelgänger: A figure that is an exact likeness or mirror image of a living person. Unlike crisis apparitions, a doppelgänger is perceived as solid in appearance for extended periods of time and traditionally associated with negative connotations. See *crisis apparition*.

dowsing: A technique used to find hidden objects, minerals, or underground water using a divining rod.

earthbound: A voluntary or involuntary condition of a ghost or spirit who continues to be perceived by the living over extended periods of time. An earthbound spirit is usually considered to be effectively "trapped" within the reality of the living.

ectoplasm: An immaterial or ethereal substance associated with spirit manifestations.

electromagnetic frequency (EMF) detector (a.k.a. magnetometer): An instrument for measuring the magnitude and direction of a magnetic field.

electronic voice phenomenon (EVP): Voices and sounds that are captured by audio recording devices. They are inaudible to the human ear, but evident upon playback.

elementals: Mythical creatures associated with elements of earth, air, water, and fire.

exorcism: A religious ritual to remove and banish an entity (or entities) believed to possess the body of a human being or animal.

extrasensory perception (ESP): Communication or perception by means other than the five accepted physical senses of sight, sound, touch, taste, and smell.

false awakening: An event in which a person believes they are awake but are actually dreaming.

false positive (a.k.a. type I error): An incorrect test result that suggests particular traits or conditions are present.

Ganzfeld experiment: A parapsychology technique used to test individuals for extrasensory perception using a mild state of sensory deprivation. The "receiver" wears headphones, is in a seated position, and has a blindfold or halved Ping-Pong balls covering their eyes. A red light shines on the receiver and white or pink noise static is simultaneously played through headphones. The receiver then describes what they perceive. See *pink noise.*

ghost: A generic term referring to a disembodied soul, which can manifest as a form of apparition or supernatural entity and may resemble a deceased person or animal.

ghost hunting: An informal, often thrill-seeking survey of a purported haunted location. See *paranormal investigation.*

hallucination: The perception of sights, sounds, and smells that are not actually present.

haunting: Reoccurring ghostly phenomena associated with a location where no one is physically present. Witness experiences may include visual apparitions, doors opening and closing without natural reason, sounds of walking or running footfalls, physical objects moving without explanation (often with no physical evidence of movement), disembodied voices and other inexplicable sounds, and the appearance of shadows without sources.

hellhound (a.k.a. black shuck): A large, spectral black dog (sometimes with red glowing eyes). Its origins reside in European folklore, and many have reported encountering this elusive, sometimes threatening creature along roadways far outside urban settlements.

hot reading: A fraudulent fortune-telling reading in which the "reader" has been furnished with prior knowledge of the sitter.

hypnosis: A sleeplike state in which the subject acts only on external suggestion and may recall hidden or long-forgotten events from their life.

illusion: A delusional discrepancy between what is perceived and what is reality.

intelligent haunting: Hauntings caused by spirits that manipulate their surroundings, interact with the living, and communicate. The spirits may behave in benevolent, malevolent, or simply mischievous manners.

intuition: Knowing without the use of any rational process. Knowledge that is gained through a perceptive insight.

investigative artifact: Something observed in an investigation or experiment that is not naturally occurring.

Kirlian photography: A specific technique to photograph the aura of living people, animals, and plants.

levitation: To lift or raise a solid object without physical means, in apparent defiance of gravity.

ley lines: Theoretical lines of naturally occurring energy connecting and aligning locations of meaningful importance on the earth's surface. First posited by Alfred Watkins (1855–1935) in 1921.

life review: A flashback of a person's life, typically associated with near-death experiences. See *near-death experience*.

lucid dreaming: A dream state in which one is conscious enough to recognize that one is in the dream state and thus able to control dream events.

Marian apparitions: Events during which an image presumed to represent the Virgin Mary is perceived.

materialization: The act of forming a solid object from nothingness.

mediumship: Mediating communication between spirits of the dead and living human beings.

mesmerism (a.k.a. hypnotism): A hypnotic induction of a sleep or trance state.

metaphysics: A branch of philosophy that studies the first principles of being, identity and change, space and time, causality, necessity, and possibility. It includes questions about the nature of consciousness and the relationship between mind and matter.

motor automatism: Bodily movement or functions that may occur subconsciously.

near-death experience (NDE): An event that is reported by people who clinically die or come close to actual death and are revived. These events often include encounters with spirit guides, seeing dead relatives or friends, life review, and out-of-body experiences.

occultism: Supernatural beliefs and practices that generally fall outside the scope of mainstream religion and science; includes the study of a wide range of phenomena involving mysticism, mesmerism, spirituality, and magic.

old hag syndrome: A nocturnal phenomenon that involves a feeling of immobilization, suffocation, odd smells, and feelings of a presence and great fear. This subject is highly controversial, as sleep paralysis may cause the same symptoms.

orb: A photographed anomaly that theoretically represents the spirit of a deceased person. Rarely seen at the time the photo is taken. Orb photographs are hotly contested, as many attribute orb images to dust particles, atmospheric moisture, flying insects, light reflection, and lens flare.

Ouija board: The original patented name by Parker Brothers Toy Company (USA) of commercially sold spirit boards. See *spirit board*.

out-of-body experience (OBE): A sensation or experience in which a living person separates from their physical body and travels to a different location. See *astral projection*.

paranormal: Referring to something that is beyond the range of normal, commonly accepted human knowledge, experience, or scientific explanation.

paranormal investigation: A scientifically controlled research project in which various methods, equipment, and experiments are used to investigate sites and reports of ghosts and hauntings.

parapsychology: The study of phenomena deemed inexplicable by conventional science.

pareidolia: Seeing familiar objects or patterns in otherwise random or unrelated objects or patterns. Pareidolia is a form of apophenia, in which people have a tendency to seek patterns in random information.

pendulum: A weighted object hanging plumb at the end of a chain or string that rotates clockwise or counterclockwise, indicating yes or no answers when used in the context of a paranormal investigation.

phantom: An image of a person or object that is seen, heard, or sensed but has no physical basis in perceived reality. See *specter*.

pink noise (a.k.a. fractal noise): An audible frequency spectrum resembling the sound of a waterfall. Commonly associated with biological systems.

poltergeist: German term meaning "noisy ghost." This is popularly believed to be a nonhuman entity or energy that is usually found to be more malicious and destructive than ghosts of deceased human beings. Phenomena normally associated with poltergeist activity include raps, knocks and banging, levitating or the moving of objects, stone-throwing, and fire-starting. It is widely believed that poltergeist activity may be associated with subconscious thought or telekinetic energy projected by women under the age of twenty-five.

portal: In paranormal terms, a theoretical doorway, entrance or gate connecting physical reality to alternate dimensions or realms. Sometime referred to as a wormhole. See *vortex*.

precognition: The ability to predict or have knowledge of something in advance of its occurrence. This may also be considered a premonition.

psi: The twenty-third letter of the Greek alphabet. It denotes psychic phenomena.

psychic: A person who displays abilities associated with psi and "sixth sense" phenomena. See *sixth sense.*

psychic photography: The result of an independent spirit energy or psi source (e.g., telepathy) with the ability to imprint images of people, animals, or objects onto photographic media. This can be achieved using both exposed and unexposed film.

psychokinesis (PK): The power of the mind to affect matter without physical contact.

psychometry: The ability to receive information concerning people or events associated with an object solely by touching or being in close proximity to it.

pyrokinesis: The ability to unconsciously control and sometimes (in rare cases) produce fire using one's mind.

random number generator (RNG): Used in psychic experimentation, this device produces numbers or symbols that cannot be predicted to appear beforehand.

recurrent spontaneous psychokinesis (RSPK): A term coined by William G. Roll to denote poltergeist phenomena. See *poltergeist.*

reincarnation: The belief that a person or animal that passes from this life is reborn into a new physical life. This idea is derived from numerous case reports of past-life memories, some involving xenoglossy. See *xenoglossy*.

remote viewing: Method used by some psychics to investigate or glean information and to travel to distant, often unknown locations by utilizing ESP. See *extrasensory perception*.

residual haunting: Observed or recorded haunting activity that does not appear to display any intelligence or ability to respond to outside stimuli.

scrying: A method used to see past, present, or future events by utilizing the still surface of a pool of water (or ink), a crystal ball, or a mirror.

séance: A meeting or gathering of people, usually lead by a medium, to communicate with the dead or receive spiritualistic messages or physical manifestations.

shadow person/figure: A nondescript dark gray or black figure, usually human-shaped, often seen from the corner of one's eye (peripheral vision). Some believe these figures represent extreme manifestations of evil, while others theorize they are entities from an alternate dimension or reality.

shaman: A member of certain tribal societies who acts as a medium between the visible world and an invisible spirit world, and who practices magic or sorcery for purposes of healing, divination, and control over natural events.

sixth sense: A theoretical keen intuitive ability outside the commonly used sense perceptions of sight, hearing, smelling, touching and tasting. Most people refer to this sensation as "gut instinct."

specter: An alternate term for a ghostly apparition or phantom.

spirit board: A flat surface displaying the alphabet and the numbers zero to nine; some include words such as *yes, no, hello,* and *goodbye.* They are used to receive spirit communications. Typically, a planchette (or pointer), an upturned glass, or a pendulum is employed to spell out words and point out numbers or letters in response to the users' questions. See *Ouija board.*

spiritualism: A nineteenth- and twentieth-century belief system and religion based on the idea that the dead are able to communicate with the living through an intermediary or medium.

stigmata: Unexplained bodily marks, sores, or sensations of pain corresponding in location to the Crucifixion wounds of Christ.

Stone Tape theory: A theory that the appearance of ghosts and haunting phenomena is the result of past traumatic events recorded or impressed onto an environment, effectively "recorded" by organic materials (such as rock) and replayed by gifted percipients under certain conditions. Also known as *place memory,* this theory was popularized in the 1972 BBC film *The Stone Tape.*

subjective apparitions: Hallucinations of apparitions or other phenomena that are created by our own minds.

subliminal perception: Sensory impressions below the threshold of conscious awareness.

supernatural: A term meaning existence outside the known, natural world. As opposed to *paranormal*, the term *supernatural* often refers to divine or demonic intervention.

synchronicity: Meaningful coincidences that are often mediated by subconscious psi activity.

tarot cards: A set of pictograph cards used by fortune-tellers to help predict future events. Some mediums utilize tarot cards to glean or clarify information on a haunted site that they are receiving psychically.

telekinesis: The movement of physical objects using one's mind.

telepathy: Communication from one mind to another through means other than the accepted five senses.

teleportation: A method of transportation in which matter or information is dematerialized (usually instantaneously) at one point and recreated or relocated at another. See *apport* and *asport*.

thought form: An apparition produced solely by the power of the human mind.

time slip: A profound change in the physical surroundings that suggests the time period being observed is not the witness's current time period but one from the past or future.

trance: A hypnotic or cataleptic state in which one becomes detached from their physical surroundings.

vortex: Believed to be an energy field that produces an opening or doorway between the physical world and nonphysical realities. See *portal*.

white noise: An acoustical or electrical sound with an intensity that is identical at all frequencies within a given frequency band or range.

xenoglossy: A phenomenon in which a person spontaneously demonstrates an ability to communicate in a language they could not have acquired by natural means.

Zener cards: A set of twenty-five cards (five each of five symbols: a hollow pointed star, a hollow circle, a plus sign, a hollow square, and three vertical wavy lines) used for testing for ESP.

RESOURCES

Highly Recommended Books

Auerbach, Loyd. *Ghost Hunting: How to Investigate the Paranormal.* Ronin Publishing, 2004.

Aykroyd, Peter H. *A History of Ghosts: The True Story of Séances, Mediums, Ghosts, and Ghostbusters.* Rodale, 2009.

Barrett, Sir William F. *On the Threshold of the Unseen: An Examination of the Phenomena of Spiritualism and of the Evidence for Survival After Death.* E. P. Dutton, 1917.

Bayless, Raymond. *Apparitions and Survival of Death.* University Books, 1973.

Bayless, Raymond. *Voices from Beyond.* University Books, 1976.

Beauregard, Mario, and Denyse O'Leary. *The Spiritual Brain: A Neuroscientist's Case for the Existence of the Soul.* HarperCollins, 2007.

Becker, Carl B. *Paranormal Experience and Survival of Death.* State University of New York Press, 1993.

Becker, Robert O., and Gary Selden. *The Body Electric: Electromagnetism and the Foundation of Life*. Quill, 1985.

Bond, Frederick Bligh. *The Gate of Remembrance» The Story of the Psychological Experiment Which Resulted in the Discovery of the Edgar Chapel at Glastonbury*. B. H. Blackwell, 1918.

Broughton, Richard S. *Parapsychology: The Controversial Science*. Ballantine Books, 1991.

Buckland, Raymond. *Doors to Other Worlds: A Practical Guide to Communicating with Spirits*. Llewellyn Publications, 1993.

Carrington, Hereward, and Nandor Fodor. *Haunted People: Story of the Poltergeist Down the Centuries*. The New American Library, 1951.

Carter, Chris. *Science and Psychic Phenomena: The Fall of the House of Skeptics*. Inner Traditions, 2012.

Casti, John L. *Paradigms Lost: Images of Man in the Mirror of Science*. Morrow, 1989.

Cornell, Tony. *Investigating the Paranormal*. Parapsychology Foundation, 2006.

Covina, Gina. *The Ouija Book*. Simon and Schuster, 1979.

Crawford, W. J. *Experiments in Psychical Science: Levitation, Contact, and the Direct Voice*. E. P. Dutton, 1919.

Crawford, W. J. *The Reality of Psychic Phenomena: Raps, Levitations, Etc.* John M. Watkins, 1916.

Crowe, Catherine. *The Night Side of Nature*. Wordsworth Editions, 2000.

Currie, Ian. *You Cannot Die: The Incredible Findings of a Century of Research on Death*. Somerville House Books, 1998.

Danelek, J. Allan. *The Case for Ghosts: An Objective Look at the Paranormal*. Llewellyn Publications, 2006.

Doyle, Arthur Conan. *The Edge of the Unknown*. J. Murray, 1930.

Findlay, Arthur. *On the Edge of the Etheric; or, Survival after Death Scientifically Explained*. Psychic Press, 1931.

Fodor, Nandor. *Between Two Worlds*. Parker, 1964.

Fodor, Nandor. *Encyclopaedia of Psychic Science*. University Books, 1966.

Fodor, Nandor. *The Haunted Mind: A Psychoanalyst Looks at the Supernatural*. The New American Library, 1968.

Ford, Arthur. *The Life Beyond Death*. Putnam, 1971.

Goode, Erich. *The Paranormal: Who Believes, Why They Believe, and Why It Matters*. Prometheus Books, 2012.

Green, Andrew. *Ghost Hunting: A Practical Guide*. Granada, 1976.

Greenhouse, Herbert B. *In Defense of Ghosts*. Essandess Special Editions, 1970.

Hill, Douglas, and Pat Williams. *The Supernatural*. Hawthorn Books, 1965.

Holzer, Hans. *Born Again: The Truth About Reincarnation*. Doubleday, 1970.

Howitt, William. *The History of the Supernatural: In All Ages and Nations and In All Churches, Christian and Pagan: Demonstrating a Universal Faith*. Longman, Green, Longman, Roberts, and Green, 1863.

Hufford, David J. *The Terror That Comes in the Night: An Experience-Centered Study of Supernatural Assault Traditions.* University of Pennsylvania Press, 1982.

Hunt, Stoker. *Ouija: The Most Dangerous Game.* Harper and Row, 1985.

Hyslop, James H. *Psychical Research and Survival.* G. Bell and Sons, 1913.

Inglis, Brian. *Science and Parascience: A History of the Paranormal, 1914–1939.* Hodder and Stoughton, 1984.

Jürgenson, Friedrich. *Voice Transmissions with the Deceased.* Firework Edition, 2004.

Kardec, Allan. *The Book on Mediums: Guide for Mediums and Invocators.* Colby and Rich, 1861.

Kurtz, Paul, ed. *A Skeptic's Handbook of Parapsychology.* Prometheus Books, 1985.

Leonard, Gladys Osborne. *My Life in Two Worlds.* Cassell, 1931.

MacKenzie, Andrew. *Hauntings and Apparitions.* Heinemann, 1982.

McAdams, Elizabeth E., and Raymond Bayless. *The Case for Life After Death: Parapsychologists Look at the Evidence.* Nelson-Hall, 1981.

Melton, J. Gordon. *Encyclopedia of Occultism and Parapsychology.* Vol. 2, 4th ed. Gale Group, 1996.

Moody, Raymond A., and Paul Perry. *Paranormal: My Life in Pursuit of the Afterlife*. HarperCollins, 2012.

Moody, Raymond A., and Paul Perry. *Reunions: Visionary Encounters with Departed Loved Ones*. Villard Books, 1993.

Osis, Kārlis, and Erlendur Haraldsson. *At the Hour of Death*. Avon, 1977.

Owen, George, and Victor Sims. *Science and the Spook: Eight Strange Cases of Haunting*. Garrett Publications, 1971.

Owen, Robert Dale. *Footfalls on the Boundary of Another World*. J. B. Lippincott, 1859.

Palmisano, Richard. *Ghosts: An Investigation into a True Canadian Haunting*. Dundurn Press, 2009.

Palmisano, Richard. *Ghosts of the Canadian National Exhibition*. Dundurn Press, 2011.

Palmisano, Richard. *Journeys into the Unknown: Mysterious Canadian Encounters with the Paranormal*. Dundurn Group, 2006.

Palmisano, Richard. *Meeting Place of the Dead: A True Haunting*. Dundurn Press, 2014.

Palmisano, Richard. *Overshadows: An Investigation into a Terrifying Modern Canadian Haunting*. Dundurn Press, 2003.

Parsons, Steven T. *Ghostology: The Art of the Ghost Hunter*. White Crow Books, 2015.

Paul, Philip. *Some Unseen Power: Diary of a Ghost-Hunter*. Robert Hale, 1985.

Peirce, Penney. *Frequency: The Power of Personal Vibration*. Atria Books, 2009.

Podmore, Frank. *Apparitions and Thought-Transference: An Examination of the Evidence for Telepathy*. Walter Scott, 1894.

Price, Harry. *The Most Haunted House in England*. Longmans, Green, 1940.

Raudive, Konstantin. *Breakthrough: An Amazing Experiment in Electronic Communication with the Dead*. Edited by Joyce Morton. Smythe, 1971.

Rhine, J. B. *New Frontiers of the Mind: The Story of the Duke Experiments*. Farrar and Rinehart, 1937.

Rhine, Louisa. *Hidden Channels of the Mind*. George J. McLeod, 1961.

Roberts, Jane. *The Seth Material*. Prentice-Hall, 1970.

Roe, Peter J. *Haunted Town Halls: From the Case Files of The Searcher Group*. Quagmire Press, 2018.

Rogo, D. Scott. *An Experience of Phantoms*. Taplinger, 1974.

Rogo, D. Scott, and Raymond Bayless. *Phone Calls from the Dead*. Prentice-Hall, 1979.

Schoch, Robert M., and Logan Yonavjak. *The Parapsychology Revolution: A Concise Anthology of Paranormal and Psychical Research*. Penguin Group, 2008.

Stein, James D. *The Paranormal Equation: A New Scientific Perspective on Remote Viewing, Clairvoyance, and Other Inexplicable Phenomena*. The Career Press, 2013.

Stirling, A. M. W. *Ghosts Vivisected: An Impartial Inquiry into Their Manners, Habits, Mentality, Motives, and Physical Construction.* Citadel Press, 1958.

Sullivan, J. W. N. *The Limitations of Science.* The New American Library, 1953.

Talbot, Michael. *Beyond the Quantum.* Bantam Books, 1988.

Terrell, Gabriel Stowe, and John Edward Terrell. *Understanding the Human Mind: Why You Shouldn't Trust What Your Brain Is Telling You.* Routledge, 2020.

Thurston, Herbert. *Ghosts and Poltergeists.* Burns, Oates, 1953.

Underhill, A. Leah. *The Missing Link in Modern Spiritualism.* Thomas R. Knox, 1885.

Underwood, Peter. *Deeper into the Occult.* Harrap, 1975.

Underwood, Peter. *The Ghost Hunter's Guide.* Javelin Books, 1988.

Underwood, Peter. *No Common Task: The Autobiography of a Ghost-Hunter.* Harrap, 1983.

Waters, Colin. *Sexual Hauntings Through the Ages.* Dorset Press, 1993.

Watson, Lyall. *Supernature: The Natural History of the Supernatural.* Hodder and Stoughton, 1973.

Watt, Caroline. *Parapsychology: A Beginner's Guide.* Oneworld Publications, 2016.

Wilson, Colin. *Mysteries: An Investigation into the Occult, the Paranormal, and the Supernatural.* Hodder and Stoughton, 1978.

Wilson, Colin. *The Occult: The Ultimate Book for Those Who Would Walk with the Gods*. Hodder and Stoughton, 1971.

Wilson, Ian. *The After Death Experience: The Physics of the Non-Physical*. Corgi Books, 1989.

Websites

Ancestry – ancestry.com/ancestry.ca

This is the largest for-profit genealogy company in the world. Historical records, births, deaths, marriages, ship voyages, family trees, and military records can be found here. Most libraries have their own Ancestry accounts that can be accessed free of charge. Do note that there are legal limitations placed on opening specific records; depending on which country you are working from, there may be a seventy-two-year (United States) or seventy-five-year (Canada) period of unobtainable data collection allowed from the date you are researching.

Internet Archive – archive.org

This is an incredibly useful source of long out-of-print books and back issues of the Society for Psychical Research and the American Society for Psychical Research. It can be accessed free of charge.

ScienceOpen – scienceopen.com

This website provides researchers with a wide range of tools to support their research; it is also free of charge.

The Searcher Group – thesearchergroup.ca

This is another incredibly useful pro bono source.

Internet-Accessible Videos

"Ghost Activity Caught on Surveillance." TheSearcherGroup. November 14, 2025. https://www.youtube.com/watch?v =EQWALLKTI7w&t=2s.

"Ghost Hunting Flashlight Trick: Physical Explanation and Experiments." verklagekasper. March 25, 2012. https://www .youtube.com/watch?v=wqNwGeXTQJk.

"Life After Death – Scientific Evidence | An Interview with Oliver Lazar." Thanatos TV EN. January 6, 2022. https://www .youtube.com/watch?v=9e1SLF7Kg8Y.

"The Meeting Place (BRTV Documentary) Humber College." Continuality. April 27, 2014. https://www.youtube.com /watch?v=4wZ1EGQyR9k.

"The Searcher Group YouTube Playlist." TheSearcherGroup. https://www.youtube.com/playlist?list=PLXqVwrcCLm _S3b3hCasXraQIyPAXvfLZx.

"Tunnel Ghosts of Fort George Pt. 1." Peter Roe. October 1, 2015. https://www.youtube.com/watch?v=9a1tvKye624.

"Tunnel Ghosts of Fort George Pt. 2." Peter Roe. October 19, 2015. https://www.youtube.com/watch?v=__MbzxZce9M.

BIBLIOGRAPHY

Absi, Gianna. "Is the Brain the Only Place That Stores Our Memories?" *The Nerve Blog.* Boston University, November 11, 2014. https://sites.bu.edu/ombs/2014/11/11/is-the-brain -the-only-place-that-stores-our-memories/.

Ambach, Wolfgang. "Correlations Between the EEGs of Two Spatially Separated Subjects – A Replication Study." *European Journal of Parapsychology* 23, no. 2 (2008): 131–46. https://ejp .wyrdwise.com/EJP%20v23-2.pdf.

Bayless, Raymond. "Correspondence." *The Journal of the American Society for Psychical Research* 43, no. 1 (1959): 35–38. https:// ia804504.us.archive.org/28/items/sim_journal-of-the-american -society-for-psychical-research_1959-01_43_1/sim_journal-of -the-american-society-for-psychical-research_1959-01_43 _1.pdf.

Besant, Annie, and C. W. Leadbeater. *Thought-Forms.* Theosophical Publishing Society, 1905.

Braden, Gregg. *The Divine Matrix: Bridging Time, Space, Miracles, and Belief.* Hay House, 2007.

Cho, Adrian. "Quantum Experiment in Space Confirms That Reality Is What You Make It." *Science*, October 27, 2017. https://www.science.org/content/article/quantum-experiment-space-confirms-reality-what-you-make-it-0.

Cirino, Erica, and Karen Lamoreux. "Should You Be Worried about EMF Exposure?" Healthline. Updated December 8, 2023. https://www.healthline.com/health/emf.

Dagnall, Neil, Kenneth G. Drinkwater, Ciarán O'Keeffe et al. "Things That Go Bump in the Literature: An Environmental Appraisal of 'Haunted Houses.'" *Frontiers in Psychology* 11 (June 2020). https://doi.org/10.3389/fpsyg.2020.01328.

David-Neel, Alexandra. *Magic and Mystery in Tibet*. Dover Publications, 1932.

Diamond, Nicholas B., Michael J. Armson, and Brian Levine. "The Truth Is Out There: Accuracy in Recall of Verifiable Real-World Events." *Psychological Science* 31, no. 12 (2020): 1544–56. https://doi.org/10.1177/0956797620954812.

Eells, Josh. "Cleve Backster: He Talked to Plants. And They Talked Back." *New York Times Magazine*, December 22, 2013. https://archive.nytimes.com/www.nytimes.com/news/the-lives-they-lived/2013/12/21/cleve-backster/.

Fabiny, Anne. "Music Can Boost Memory and Mood." *Harvard Women's Health Watch*, February 14, 2015. https://www.health.harvard.edu/mind-and-mood/music-can-boost-memory-and-mood.

Flaxington, Beverly D. "The Ruminating Mind." *Psychology Today*, October 9, 2019. https://www.psychologytoday.com/ca/blog /understand-other-people/201910/the-ruminating-mind.

Garrigue, L., and Laurence Lecot. "A Note about Reproducibility in Visual ITC." *Institut français de recherche et d'epérimentation spirite* (2021). https://doi.org/10.31219/osf.io/8r46g.

Greyson, Bruce. "Near-Death Experiences and Systems Theories: A Biosociological Approach to Mystical States." *The Journal of Mind and Behavior* 12, no. 4 (1991): 487–508. https://med .virginia.edu/perceptual-studies/wp-content/uploads/sites /360/2017/01/NDE20.pdf.

Gritzan, Elena. "This Will Make You Believe in Ghosts." *Broadview*, October 3, 2016. https://broadview.org/this-will-make-you -believe-in-ghosts/.

Guiley, Rosemary Ellen. *The Encyclopedia of Demons and Demonology*. Infobase Publishing, 2009.

"Gurwitsch (Gurvich), Alexander Gavrilovich." Encyclopedia.com. Accessed March 18, 2024. https://www.encyclopedia.com /religion/encyclopedias-almanacs-transcripts-and-maps /gurwitsch-gurvich-alexander-gavrilovich.

Haslam, Garth. "1966: The Shadow's Ghost." Accessed February 25, 2025. http://anomalyinfo.com/Stories/1966-ghost-gay-street.

"Institute of Noetic Sciences (IONS)." Accessed February 25, 2025. https://noetic.org.

Ishida, Masayoshi. "Rebuttal to Claimed Refutations of Duncan MacDougall's Experiment on Human Weight Change at the Moment of Death." *Journal of Scientific Exploration* 24, no. 1 (2010): 5–39.

Itani, Omar. "You Are What You Think: How Your Thoughts Create Your Reality." April 21, 2020. https://www.omaritani .com/blog/what-you-think.

Kraig, Donald Michael. "Term: Kirlian Photography." Llewellyn. Accessed February 25, 2025. http://www.llewellyn .com/encyclopedia/term/Kirlian+Photography.

MacDougall, Duncan. "Hypothesis Concerning Soul Substance." *Journal of the American Society for Psychical Research* 1, no. 5 (1907): 237–44. https://diogenesii.wordpress.com/wp-content /uploads/2014/04/duncan_macdougall_1907_-_21pp.pdf.

Mainwood, Paul. "Einstein Believed in a Theory of Spacetime That Can Help People Cope with Loss." *Forbes*. Updated June 30, 2021. https://www.forbes.com/sites/quora/2016/12/28 /einstein-believed-in-a-theory-of-spacetime-that-can-help -people-cope-with-loss/?sh=7896686555d2.

Martin, Boyd. "Your DNA Communicates with Light." Quantum Health News, July 14, 2020. https://pureenergyrx.com/blogs /pure-energy-rx-blog/quantum-health-news-july-2020.

McCue, Peter A. "Theories of Haunting: A Critical Overview." *The Journal of the Society for Psychical Research* 661, no. 866 (2002): 1–21. sgha.net/library/theories-of-hauntings.pdf.

McLeod, Saul. "Solomon Asch Conformity Line Experiment Study." SimplyPsychology. Updated October 24, 2023. https://www.simplypsychology.org/asch-conformity.html.

Moberly, Charlotte Anne Elizabeth, and Eleanor Jourdain. *An Adventure*. Macmillan, 1911.

Muro, Trisha. "Explainer: The Fundamental Forces." *ScienceNewsExplores*, April 5, 2022. https://www.snexplores .org/article/explainer-fundamental-forces-physics-gravity -electricity-magnetism-weak-strong.

Owen, Iris M., and Margaret H. Sparrow. *Conjuring Up Philip: An Adventure in Psychokinesis*. Fitzhenry & Whiteside, 1976.

Owen, Iris M., and Margaret H. Sparrow. "Generation of Paranormal Physical Phenomenon in Connection with an Imaginary Communicator." *New Horizons* 1, no. 3 (1974): 6–13. https://survivalresearch.ca/NHRF/NHJ/New_Horizons _Journal_vol_1_no_3_January_1974.pdf.

Parker, Adrian, and Annekatrin Puhle. "Thoughtforms." PSI Encyclopedia. Updated April 23, 2023. https://psi -encyclopedia.spr.ac.uk/articles/thoughtforms.

Parsons, Steven T. "Infrasound and the Paranormal." *Journal of the Society for Psychical Research* 76.3, no. 908 (2012): 150–74. https://sgha.net/library/INFRASOUND.pdf.

Persinger, Michael. "My Tectonic Strain Theory Is Alive and Well." *Sacred Pathways – Blogs in Neurotheology*, May 31, 2015. https:// sacredneurology.com/2015/05/31/the-tectonic-strain-theory -and-the-haunted-room-a-blog-by-dr-michael-persinger/.

Persinger, Michael. "The Neuropsychiatry of Paranormal Experiences." *The Journal of Neuropsychiatry and Clinical Neurosciences* 13, no. 4 (2001). https://doi.org/10.1176 /jnp.13.4.515.

Peshawaria, Rajeev. "Quantum Mechanics, Spirituality and Leadership." *Forbes.* Updated September 15, 2015. https://www.forbes.com/sites/rajeevpeshawaria/2014/03/21 /quantum-mechanics-spirituality-leadership/?sh=2dfa11ae1c2d.

Poponin, Vladimir. "The DNA Phantom Effect: Consciousness-Science Protocol 2." Updated March 19, 2002. https://www .fceia.unr.edu.ar/geii/maestria/Intercatedra/SENSUM/The %20DNA%20Phantom%20Effect.htm.

Roll, William G. *The Poltergeist.* Nelson Doubleday, 1972.

Rosin, Hanna. "Pope's Vision of Heaven, Hell Riles Evangelicals." *Washington Post.* August 16, 1999. https://www.washingtonpost .com/archive/politics/1999/08/17/popes-vision-of-heaven-hell -riles-evangelicals/ce5208c7-2bf7-4f1b-94b8-7c00ae497756/.

Schaefer, Hans-Eckhardt. "Music-Evoked Emotions—Current Studies." *Frontiers in Neuroscience* 11 (2017). https://doi .org/10.3389/fnins.2017.00600.

Shrand, Joseph A. "A Simple Technique to Manage Anxiety." *Psychology Today*, December 15, 2014. https://www .psychologytoday.com/us/blog/manage-your-stress /201412/simple-technique-manage-anxiety.

Sinneberg, Jackson. "As Exorcism Demand Continues to Rise, Vatican to Hold Training." The National Desk. Updated February 28, 2023. https://thenationaldesk.com/news

/americas-news-now/vatican-to-hold-training-next-month
-as-demand-for-exorcism-continues-to-rise-catholic-church
-prayer-ritual-priests-internation-association-of-exorcists
-paranormal-supernatural-psychiatry-mental-health.

"Society for Psychical Research." Accessed February 25, 2025.
https://www.spr.ac.uk/home.

Stevenson, Ian. "The Contribution of Apparitions to the Evidence
for Survival." *Journal of the American Society for Psychical Research*
76 (1982): 341–58. https://med.virginia.edu/perceptual-studies
/wp-content/uploads/sites/360/2017/09/The-Contributions
-of-Apparitions-to-the-Evidence-for-Survival_-Ian
-Stevenson-1982.pdf.

Tandy, Vic. "The Ghost in the Machine." *Journal of the Society for
Psychical Research* 62, no. 851 (1998).

Tiller, William A. "What Are Subtle Energies?" *Journal of Scientific
Exploration* 7, no. 3 (1993): 293–304. https://citeseerx.ist.psu
.edu/viewdoc/download?doi=10.1.1.548.2332&rep=rep1
&type=pdf.

Tressoldi, Patrizio E. "Extraordinary Claims Require Extraordinary
Evidence: The Case of Non-Local Perception, a Classical and
Bayesian Review of Evidences." *Frontiers in Psychology* 2, no. 117
(2011). https://doi.org/10.3389/fpsyg.2011.00117.

Volodyaev, Ilya, and Lev V. Beloussov. "Revisiting the Mitogenetic
Effect of Ultra-Weak Photon Emission." *Frontiers in Physiology* 6
(2015). https://doi:10.3389/fphys.2015.00241.

"What Is the Rhine?" The Rhine. Accessed February 25, 2025.
https://www.rhineonline.org/about-us.

ABOUT THE AUTHORS

Richard Palmisano

Raised in a haunted house, Richard's memories of things going bump in the night started around four years of age, which he believes nudged him into a lifelong exploration of all things strange. His passion for solving mysteries pushed him onto two equally demanding paths: the first was a long-time career into security and law enforcement, and second was the founding of The Searcher Group (1979), fulfilling his quest to find answers to the afterlife. Sometimes these two paths collided with remarkable results, as Richard's credentials allowed him to go where most could not. Over many years Richard has been honored to have five books published documenting investigations he's conducted. Though many have asked why he has not written more books, his answer is that not every haunting merits one; only those exceptional stories that help advance our understanding of life after death and open our minds to possibilities inspires Richard to put pen to paper.

Richard can be reached at richard@thesearchergroup.ca.

Peter J. Roe

As assistant director to Richard and The Searcher Group, Peter is also director of TSG subdivision Mortal Coil Paranormal (MCP), serving the Greater Toronto Area and southwestern Ontario. A veteran of Canadian television animation by trade and author of *Rock & Rule: The Art and Story of a Cult Film* (RAID Press, projected release 2026), Peter dedicates much of his spare time to the meaningful pursuit of educating the public on paranormal phenomena and advocating for Ontario's vanishing, oft unappreciated heritage through acquiring the stories relayed by its ghosts. *The Complete Paranormal Investigation Handbook* marks Peter's second publication endeavor concerning ghost phenomena studies following the worldwide release of *Haunted Town Halls* (Quagmire Press) in 2018. Peter is currently in the throes of writing two more ghost-related works.

For paranormal matters, Peter can be reached at mortalcoil paranormal@gmail.com.

To Write to the Authors

If you wish to contact the authors or would like more information about this book, please write to the authors in care of Llewellyn Worldwide Ltd. and we will forward your request. Both the authors and publisher appreciate hearing from you and learning of your enjoyment of this book and how it has helped you. Llewellyn Worldwide Ltd. cannot guarantee that every letter written to the authors can be answered, but all will be forwarded. Please write to:

Richard Palmisano
Peter J. Roe
℅ Llewellyn Worldwide
2143 Wooddale Drive
Woodbury, MN 55125-2989

Please enclose a self-addressed stamped envelope for reply,
or $1.00 to cover costs. If outside the U.S.A., enclose
an international postal reply coupon.

Many of Llewellyn's authors have websites with additional information and resources. For more information, please visit our website at http://www.llewellyn.com.

Notes

Notes

Notes

Notes

Notes

Notes

Notes